Wisdom of the Stars

Wisdom of the Stars

Astrology and Spiritual Biography

Leo de la Houssaye

Floris Books

Translated by Lynda Hepburn

First published in German as
Auf dem Wege zu einer neuen Sternenweisheit by
Verlag am Goetheanum, Dornach, Switzerland in 2007.
First published in English by Floris Books in 2011.

British Library CIP Data available
ISBN 978-086315-799-8
Printed in Great Britain
by CPI Antony Rowe

Contents

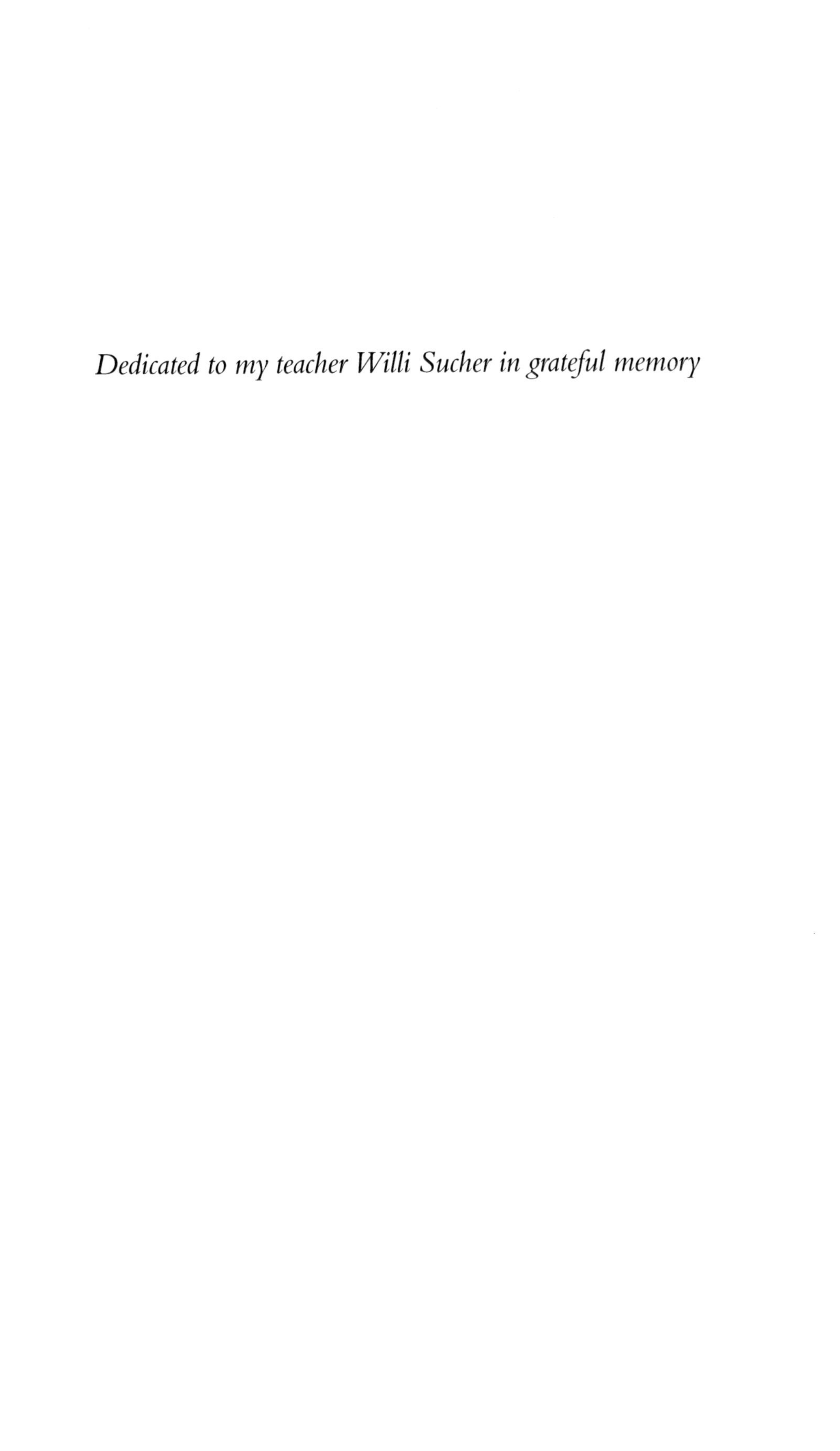

Dedicated to my teacher Willi Sucher in grateful memory

Preface

This book, requested by many listeners of lectures which I gave over the last ten years, has a long history.

In my twenties, my interest in astrology awakened a great desire to develop this area further. My encounter with anthroposophy opened up completely unexpected avenues. Later, a crucial meeting with Willi Sucher (1902–85) pointed me in the right direction. From 1969 onwards the conversations with him laid the basis for the approach described here and the ensuing mode of observing celestial phenomena. My path led me to the perception of relationships between man and the stars which I would not have considered possible previously.

As mentioned, the content of the following chapters has developed over many years as the fruit of lectures in numerous countries. I have not attempted to give a complete description of all the developmental possibilities of a new wisdom of the stars. This book is not intended to be a textbook but rather a source above all to motivate the reader to carry out their own research. The intention is to make the reader aware of relationships between man and the world of the stars which are almost never considered nowadays because they are not expected.

The observations described here can only be understood properly by means of Rudolf Steiner's anthroposophy. Familiarity with the fundamentals of anthroposophy are therefore necessary, in particular that the mystery of Golgotha is the key turning point in the evolution of mankind and that the relationship of man to the world of stars received a fundamentally new orientation through this event.

The present-day materialistic picture of the cosmos shaped by space travel is so dominant in human consciousness that the contemplation of the sky as described here is viewed as unscientific. It is becoming increasingly necessary and urgent to demonstrate that nowadays a completely new way of viewing the stars is possible through anthroposophy.

I would like to thank the many friends who have listened to my lectures, who have encouraged me to write down the results of my research and have given assistance with this process.

I hope that this book will find unbiased open-minded readers who will be motivated to their own further study and search for the truth.

Leo de la Houssaye

1. The Beginnings of a Wisdom of the Stars

Nowadays anyone who opens an astrology book with the question: 'what is astrology?' often finds the answer: 'astrology is an ancient knowledge dating from earliest times, an ancient wisdom which has been passed down for thousands of years.'

This might give the impression that astrology is something which has remained unchanged for thousands of years and has not undergone any development. However, the opposite is true: astrology has definitely undergone significant development.

This development can be looked at in the light of anthroposophy. From an anthroposophical viewpoint human development takes place in stages through cultural epochs. These epochs each last around 2160 years. This number is the cosmic number of a 'world month,' the twelfth part of a Platonic Year (25,920 years), in the course of which the spring equinox travels once through the whole zodiac.

The following periods are important for a historical examination of astrology:

— the Egyptian-Babylonian-Chaldean cultural epoch. This began around 2900 BC and lasted until the founding of Rome (*c.* 750 BC);

— the Greco-Roman cultural epoch which lasted from *c.* 750 BC until the beginning of the fifteenth century;

— our present day cultural epoch which will last until around the year 3550.

In each of these epochs the wisdom of the stars assumed a form suited to the epoch. Because the manifestations of star wisdom were very different in these epochs and because the word 'astrology' generally makes us think of the present-day form, in what follows the generic term 'star wisdom' will be used for what appeared in very different ways in the different cultural epochs.

In the course of the cultural epochs referred to, mankind underwent a spiritual development. During the Egyptian-Babylonian-Chaldean epoch the sentient soul developed, during the Greco-Roman epoch the intellectual or mind soul developed and in our present-day cultural epoch the consciousness soul is developing. This evolution of the soul has been described so often that a short explanation should suffice here.[1]

The world was filled with meaning for the sentient soul. The world of the stars was viewed as an expression of the world of the gods. Man turned his gaze upwards to the stars and said to himself, 'What the stars reveal is an expression of the ruling gods, a text which the gods have written. What can be perceived by the senses in the world of the stars is a revelation of the gods.'

In the Greco-Roman cultural epoch which followed, the development of the intellectual or mind soul took place. This involved a process of internalization. The human being began to think for himself: he developed reason. The world no longer spoke directly to human beings, but the human being began to think about and interpret the phenomena of the world including the world of the stars himself. The love of thinking, *philo-sophia,* arose in the Greek civilization, the experience of the self as an independent citizen in the Roman one.

In the present-day cultural epoch of the development of the consciousness soul, the process of human independence is progressing still further. The self is awakening in the soul. The human being is becoming skilled on earth and changing the world through the development of technology. He has to take on responsibility for his actions, responsibility towards his fellow human beings, towards the world and towards the cosmos. The consciousness soul is the soul of responsibility.

We are only at the start of this period: two thirds still lie ahead.

The dark age

The question is often asked about mankind's nature before the soul began to evolve. In the most ancient times the soul life was not individualized. Human beings still lived completely in unity with their environment and this environment was experienced as a spiritual reality. The people of that time possessed clairvoyant abilities. They could perceive spiritual beings and lived in very close contact with this spiritual world.

If a storm was raging, then the storm gods were at work. River gods lived in the river, water beings in the rippling streams and fountain spirits in the springs. In this way the activity of elemental beings was experienced in nature.

The world of the stars was also inhabited by spiritual beings. When human beings turned their gaze upwards to the starry sky they experienced the star gods.

In the most ancient times the earthly world still had little meaning: only the spiritual world was a reality.

In the course of time mankind lost these clairvoyant faculties. Human beings no longer associated with the spiritual beings in nature and in the stars as a matter of course.

An important transition in this was the dawning of Kali Yuga, the dark age. It began around 3100 BC and lasted for 5000 years. A 'twilight of the gods' set in. From then on human consciousness gradually took leave of the spiritual world. A darkening of consciousness in relation to the spiritual world set in: the old natural clairvoyance began to fade. During the dark age it was replaced by a clear alert consciousness of the world of the senses.

This development was necessary in order to make human beings independent, to make them into free beings. As long as mankind lived amongst spiritual beings he could never become free. To do this his consciousness had to take leave of the spiritual realities, he had to develop from a 'heavenly' being into a citizen of the earth.

This separation from the world of spiritual beings is described in the Bible in the picture of the Fall. The expulsion from paradise had far-reaching consequences for human existence. The effects of this event spanned long periods of time. One outcome of this event was the dark age.

This stage was connected to a developmental process in the human being: the contracting of the human etheric body.

The old clairvoyant consciousness arose because the human being's etheric body had a certain independence from the physical body. During the Atlantean time the etheric body projected far beyond the physical body. Even in later times when the physical body became increasingly dense and hard, the human being retained the ability from Atlantean times of being a giant. From an etheric point of view the human being was far larger than his physical body. Because his etheric body projected beyond the physical body, he possessed clairvoyant faculties, a natural clairvoyance.

When the dark age dawned a process of contraction began in the etheric body. The etheric body began to adapt to the form of the physical body. In particular, the etheric head gradually came to coincide with the physical head.

This not only gave rise to a completely new consciousness but also to a completely new awareness of life. The human being suddenly experienced himself as being closely connected to his bodily nature, as though incarcerated in a house that was too small. He felt himself to be an inconsequential earthly human being, alienated from the spiritual world, from heaven.

A great desire awoke to find the way back to heaven. The human being wanted to be larger than he was and therefore to build a larger body externally. A tremendous desire to build arose, an architectural desire. People were aware that they could no longer be giants. The urge to be a giant sought fulfilment in the creation of huge buildings.[2] In Egypt the gigantic pyramids arose suddenly around 3000 BC. In Mesopotamia at the same time stepped tower-like pyramids were built, the ziggurats. As a building design the ziggurat is as characteristic of Mesopotamia as the pyramids are of Egypt.

At this time human beings felt themselves to be abruptly alienated from the world of the stars. A deep longing awoke to find the lost world of the stars again. The search for the wisdom of the stars arose. This search did not exist before the dawning of the dark age. The revelations of the world of the stars were a given for mankind through their innate clairvoyance. The quest for knowledge of the stars only began at the moment when mankind started to lose its ability to perceive the world of the stars.

The origins of a wisdom of the stars therefore began at the start of the third millennium BC in two places: Egypt and Mesopotamia.

Before examining these origins, mention should be made of observation of the sky and interpretation of the calendar as preliminary stages in a wisdom of the stars.

Observation of the sky and interpretation of the calendar

Human beings have lived with the rhythms of the heavens through all ages: the rhythms of day and night, the rhythm of the seasons. The rising and setting of the Sun was experienced as a meaningful event. The Moon was also an important phenomenon for some peoples. It was noticed how the Moon first appears in the evening sky as a thin sickle and then increases in size until it is visible the whole night as a full Moon. And how it then wanes until it disappears again as a thin sickle in the morning sky.

All peoples have distinguished constellations in the sky and given them names. The night sky was observed because this is essential for orientation on the earth.

— We orientate ourselves in *space* according to the points of the compass: east, west, north, south. These spatial directions are determined by cosmic phenomena of sunrise, sunset, and the pole star around which the stars rotate.
— We orientate ourselves in *time* by days, months, years. These are units of time which are connected to the Sun, Moon and stars.

The human being cannot orientate himself on the earth without being able to see the sky phenomena. All orientation in space and time derives from the cosmos. Even the word 'orientate' is based on the orient, that is, the east.

In the earliest times from which records survive the *spatial* environment was perceived as divine: the gods were at work in nature. Contact with nature was contact with spiritual beings.

Time was also experienced as divine. Time was not experienced as measurable quantitative time, but periods of time (such as morning, noon, evening, night, spring, summer, autumn, winter) which were significantly different in quality because they were connected to different spiritual beings. Gods were at work in the element of time. The only known time was 'sacred time.'

Cosmic rhythms were experienced as having meaning. They were not accidental but determined by the gods. The first calendars were created in order to be able to orientate according to the time gods. The creation of the calendar was a matter for the priests. Not only because the necessary knowledge was reserved for them but because a life oriented by the calendar was actually an act of worship — living with the gods of time.

In the most ancient times it was usually the lunar calendar based on the phases of the Moon which was used. According to this the lunar month (phases) had 29 or 30 days. For some peoples the beginning of the lunar month was marked by the disappearance of the Moon at dawn. However, for the Babylonians the lunar month began with the appearance of the new sickle Moon in the evening. The new lunar cycle was solemnly announced there by the chief priests. The word 'calendar' is still a reminder of this *calare:* announcing, proclaiming the new month in ancient Rome.

Besides the lunar calendar, the ancient Egyptians knew of the 365-day year at a very early date (*c.* 3000 BC). From this they produced 36 'weeks' each of ten days. The five missing days were added at the end of the year as festivals. These days served to honour the five most important gods: Osiris, Isis, Nephthys, Seth and Horus.

However, it was not the Sun that was used to determine the length of the year but the fixed stars, the heliacal rising of the stars.

What does this mean? A star which is exactly in the south at midnight on a particular night will be at this point 4 minutes before 12 the following night. On the day after that it will be there 8 minutes before 12. After a month the time difference is 30 × 4 minutes, that is 2 hours, and in a whole year 24 hours. If we were to look at the sky at the same time each day, then the whole night sky would pass before our eyes once during the course of a year.

Stars which set about two hours after sunset today will set progressively earlier over the next few days and therefore fade in the twilight. The stars in question are still visible in the evening after sunset, but then disappear in the light of the setting sun. They go through a period of being invisible until they are again visible in the morning sky just before sunrise. In the ensuing days they rise earlier and earlier and are therefore visible for longer periods before the Sun rises.

Reference was made to the heliacal rising of a star when it was seen *for the first time* before sunrise after a period of invisibility. In the Egyptian civilization this event of a star becoming visible before sunrise was viewed as the 'birth of the star.'

The heliacal rising of Sirius (in Canis Major beneath Orion) marked the beginning of the new year.

Constant observation of the rhythms of Sun, Moon and stars provided the basis for the first calendar systems. Knowledge of the calendar was therefore the oldest science of sky phenomena. It was cultivated by the priests and kept secret. However, the priests not only observed the cosmic rhythms but also the will of the gods. This gave rise to calendars of religious festivals where the days had different meanings. There were festivals decreed by the gods, memorial days for the deeds of gods and days for particular ceremonies and sacrificial rituals. All these were given in the calendar. Attaching qualitative meaning to individual periods of time can be seen as a preliminary stage in astrology or the wisdom of the stars.

The religion of the stars in ancient Egypt was particularly connected to thetime periods characterized by the gods, whereas in Babylonia the emphasis was more on the interpretation of spatial sky phenomena as portents.

2. The Egyptian Star Religion

Egyptian culture was guided by the mysteries. The founder of this culture was Thot. Later renewers of ancient Egyptian wisdom also called themselves Thot in accordance with an old custom of the Egyptian sages. The Greeks called him Hermes and called the original Thot the 'Thrice Great': Hermes Trismegistus. He is viewed as the inaugurator of the Egyptian star mysteries. This gave rise to the name Hermes mysteries for the Egyptian star mysteries. The Egyptians looked on Thot as the one who had taught human beings to write. He was called the 'Lord of the Word of God,' that is, the hieroglyph writing. The mathematical sciences and geometry were also traced back to the wisdom of Thot: 'He calculates everything which is on the earth ... He calculates the time for gods and men ... He is the lord of the world of the stars.' The writing of the stars was brought down to earth by Thot in mathematics and geometry. He also taught human beings to find what was taking place on the earth in the stars.

Thot was therefore revered as the one who received inspiration from the heavenly powers. Someone living in Ancient Egypt felt him to be 'not merely a great teacher, but a being to whom he looked up with the deepest feelings of gratitude, the deepest respect, saying to himself: all that I have comes from you. You stood above in an ancient time and sent down through those who were the bearers of your teachings, that which flows into outer human culture and will become the greatest blessing for mankind.'[1]

One of the oldest texts from the Egyptian culture, recorded in a pyramid (*c.* 2400 BC) says that Sirius 'is the bringer of the new year and the flood.'[2]

The flooding of the Nile was the main natural event in ancient

Egypt. According to Herodotus, 'Egypt is a gift of the Nile.' The country owed its existence to the fertility of the soil caused by the mud from the Nile. The time of the annual flooding of this river was awaited with the greatest interest. By observing the sky it appeared as though the bright fixed star Sirius announced the rising of the Nile. When Sirius reappeared before sunrise in the morning sky for the first time after a period of being invisible, this was the sign that the Nile would burst its banks a few weeks later and make the land fertile. The heliacal rising of Sirius, the star of Isis, brought the proclamation of Isis, the goddess of fertility.

The Egyptians felt the stars to be the dwelling places of the gods. During their periods of invisibility, the gods associated with the stars spent their time in the underworld. The heliacal rising of a star meant the rebirth of a star god after they had been in the underworld.

Records survive of what are known as 'diagonal calendars.' These are lists which show which stars or groups of stars will rise heliacally during a period of ten days. This calendar gave a bearing on the world of the gods because, for each ten-day period, it showed which star gods would be reborn after their sojourn in the underworld.

The calendar had 36 columns. The first column showed star (A) which rose heliacally in a particular ten-day period. Ten days later another star (B) rose heliacally and the first star stood higher in the sky. In the next ten-day period this star rose even earlier and stood further up in the sky when the next star (C) rose heliacally. Thus the positions of the stars formed a diagonal in the series of columns.

		A
	A	B
A	B	C

These diagonal calendars were placed on the inside of the lids of coffins for mummies. They accompanied the dead into their graves. The Egyptians gave their dead a great deal for the long journey after death: food, written texts, jewellery, etc. and also diagonal calendars so that those who had died could find their way in the world of the gods.

The oldest diagonal calendars which have been found date from the period of the Middle Kingdom, from graves in Assiut and Aswan (*c.* 2000 BC) and from the grave of Senmut, the chancellor of Queen Hatshepsut (*c.* 1450 BC) in the New Kingdom.

Gods of time

The Egyptian civilization was characterized by its focus on gods of time: gods who ruled over particular periods of time. The year was divided into twelve months each of thirty days. Adding five feast days at the end of the twelve months produced the year of 365 days. Each month contained three periods of ten days. The Egyptians therefore had ten-day weeks, as it were, these being known as decades. Each period of ten days was ruled over by a decade god who was the guardian of this period.

A decade was therefore a period of ten days. The stars or constellations which rose heliacally in these decades were called decans. But the gods who were connected to these constellations were also called decans or decan gods, giving 36 of these gods.[3]

As already mentioned, time was considered to be sacred by the culture of that period. Time was something completely real and alive. Each period of time *was* a spiritual being. According to the Egyptologist Neugebauer, the most striking characteristic of Egyptian culture is this deification of time.[4] In his book *Ma'at,* Jan Assmann also makes the point that

> the Egyptian did not think of the cosmos spatially, but in terms of time. What we refer to as the 'cosmos' was viewed by the Egyptian as a process. And this process is in the first instance nothing other than life: the life of a community of gods which takes place in the endless birth and death of the cosmic cycles and above all in the path of the Sun.'[5]

The cosmos was therefore a living process in which human beings lived in community with the gods.

The view of the spatial nature of the cosmos was far less developed. The twelvefold nature of the zodiac connected with space is never mentioned in what has been handed down to us from Egyptian culture.

The work of Egyptologists gives us a fairly reliable picture of this culture. Nothing has survived from either the Old Kingdom or the Middle and New Kingdoms which indicates that the twelvefold nature of the zodiac was known. It is assumed that this was first adopted at a later date in Mesopotamia or Greece. The oldest depiction of the zodiac in Egypt first appears around 200 BC in the Temple of Khnum at Esna. The best known is that in the Temple of Hathor at Dendera.

The planets were not viewed as sacred in Egyptian culture as was often the case with other peoples. Only the Sun and Moon were worshipped as being divine. This is understandable as the Sun and Moon were connected to the calendar, that is, to the sacred nature of time.

There were other gods of time, such as the gods of the months. The twelve months bore the names of the divine guardians who were connected to these months. We only know the names of these months from Greek records, for example the first month was called Thot, the second Paophi.

These periods of time ruled by the gods were interpreted accordingly: the first month which was dedicated to Thot was favourable for all matters connected to Thot; the second month, dedicated to Paophi, was favourable for all matters connected to the god Paophi, etc.

Predictions for the day have also been handed down from the period of the nineteenth dynasty (*c.* 1300 BC) in what is known as the 'calendar of fates of good and evil days.' Each day was connected with particular events in the world of the gods. For example, on the twenty second of the (first) month of Thot, it is said regarding the creation of the world:

> Rê [the god of creation] summoned all the gods and

> goddesses and they gathered around him. He let them enter his stomach. There they began to rumble inside him and he killed them all. Then he spat them out [into the water] and they changed into fish. Their souls became birds and flew into the sky. So their bodies had changed into fish and their souls into birds ...

The rule on this day is: 'Thou shall not eat fish on this day nor burn fish oil to make light. Thou shall not eat any birds.' On the twenty second day of Thot birds and fish are under the sign of creation. Their sacred nature prohibits them being eaten as food or used for other purposes.[6]

On the 23 day of Thot it is said:

> Do not burn incense on the fire [for the god] on this day. Do not kill goats nor deer nor birds; eat neither goose nor goat on this day. Do not listen to either song or dance music. Because on this day the heart of Rê was sad because of what he had done to his children [the gods]. No child that is born on this day will live.

On the 27 day of Thot 'the reconciliation of Horus and Seth was commanded.' Therefore the calendar advised, 'kill no cattle on this day,' so that peace should not be destroyed by a bloody deed and make a sacrifice to the names of these two gods.

Every piece of advice and prediction was therefore connected to the events in the world of the gods.

The Greek historian Herodotus travelled widely and spent an extended period in Egypt. There he became familiar with the Egyptian manner of interpretation described here which was unknown at the time in Greece. Herodotus reported: 'The Egyptians also have the notion of which god is holy in each month and day; which destiny someone will have depending on the day of his birth, how he will end and what he will become afterwards.' Herodotus was amazed at the kind of 'astrology' which was not based on observation of phenomena in the sky but on interpretation of the periods ruled over by the gods. The predictions were universal and applied to all human beings.

This interpretation based on chronology is also called chronomancy. All predictions for auspicious and inauspicious days from later times go back to the ancient Egyptian deification of time and its time gods.

The decan predictions (for ten-day periods) also arose from interpretation of the constellations heliacally rising during a ten-day period and their decan gods. This interpretation of periods of time, this calendar interpretation, is characteristic of the Egyptian culture where star wisdom was associated with the element of time.

The Sothic cycle

What is known as the Sothic cycle is connected to the inner relationship that the ancient Egyptians had to chronology, to periods and rhythms of time. It played a central role in the calendar system which went back to the teachings of Hermes Trismegistus. The Egyptians worked with a year of 365 days. As is well known, the solar year has a length of about 365¼ days. We adjust for this difference by inserting a leap day every four years. But the Egyptians did not do this. Their calendar year therefore shifted in relation to the astronomical year by a day after every four years; and after 120 years by about thirty days — a month.

If our calendar were arranged like this then for example, the start of the year, New Year's Day, would move through the seasons over the course of time. Our New Year's Day in winter would gradually move into autumn, then into summer, into spring and finally return to the starting point in winter. This would happen after 1,460 (365 × 4) years, as was in fact the case in ancient Egypt. This period of 1,460 years is called a Sothic cycle.

A Sothic cycle began when the start of the year coincided with the heliacal rising of Sothis, our Sirius, which is why this period of 1,460 years is named after Sothis.

Censorinus, a Roman writer, provides evidence for the beginning of a Sothic cycle in the year AD 139. Calculating back from this year by 1,460 years gives 1322 and 2782 BC as the starting years of earlier Sothic cycles (it must be remembered that the year zero does not exist).

It is quite incorrect to say that things were organized in a stupid and impractical way in those days because the Egyptians did not know about the leap year. If they had wished to have this correction using leap days then they would certainly have done so.

In actual fact the Sothic cycles contained a spiritual reality in connection with the wisdom of the stars. Originally there was an intrinsic perception of the living star wisdom: the sublime star goddess Isis could be seen in the mysteries. However the original visionary power was gradually lost over the course of time. The power of beholding declined a step at a time with each Sothic cycle. This was the law of the Sothic cycles in connection with the wisdom of the stars which was known in the mysteries.[7]

The Sothic cycles had crucial significance for the course of Egyptian civilization. It is no coincidence that the flowering of this culture (from the first to the nineteenth dynasty) coincided exactly with a Sothic cycle (*c.* 2800 – *c.* 1300 BC). That was the time when the Egyptian star wisdom experienced a highpoint in the mysteries.

In the transition to the next Sothic cycle the living wisdom of the stars — also in the mysteries — gradually faded. We know how the Pharaoh Akhenaton made the greatest possible efforts to change the situation. But after his death (*c.* 1340 BC) the decline of the mysteries began. A spiritual emptiness, a barrenness set in.

The later pharaohs of the nineteenth dynasty attempted to cover up the spiritual desolation with the greatest efforts at ritual magic and ceremonial displays of splendour, but from then on the decline of Egyptian civilization could no longer be halted.

3. The Mesopotamian Star Religion

During the Egyptian-Babylonian-Chaldean cultural epoch the longing for the cosmos, for the world of the stars, arose in Egypt and Mesopotamia at the same time. Mesopotamia was the Greek name for the land of two rivers, the land between the Euphrates and Tigris. The developments in Egypt and Mesopotamia were as different as the two civilizations themselves.

What the two cultures had in common was the fact that, when the dark age arrived, mysteries arose at the time when human beings began to loose their connection to the spiritual world. The mysteries served the task of maintaining mankind's connection to the spiritual world.

Just as the Egyptian culture was inaugurated by Hermes Trismegistus, so Gilgamesh was the inaugurator of the outer Babylonian culture. Hermes Trismegistus was an initiate who knew the holy secrets of the mysteries. Egyptian culture was therefore a mystery culture. It was led by the mysteries and marked by their impulses. In contrast, Gilgamesh *sought* the mysteries. The epic of Gilgamesh relates how he failed to penetrate to the deepest secrets of the mysteries. In Babylonia the outer and inner esoteric cultures diverged. They were no longer one and the same thing. The Babylonian culture also possessed mysteries but these remained in the background to a greater degree.

The land of the two rivers was originally inhabited by the Sumerians, a people whose origin is historically uncertain. The Sumerians invented cuneiform script, or rather 'received it from the gods,' as the script came to earth from above. The script was originally with the gods: human beings read the star script which was written by the gods in heaven. The script was invented when the writing in the stars could no longer be read naturally, when it fell to earth so to speak.

The sign for 'god' was identical to the sign for 'star' and 'constellation' in the cuneiform script of the Sumerians. Why did these people identify their gods with stars? Their gods lived in the stars, the stars were the dwelling place of the gods. The Sumerians had a strongly developed star religion. Cuneiform writing and the star religion originated with the Sumerians and were adopted by other peoples.

The dawn of the dark age was a decisive turning point for the Sumerians. It was as though the beholding soul of light floated away. Human beings began to be citizens of the earth but at the same time a spiritual blindness came upon them. Until then culture had been inspired *from above* by the gods. Now mankind was left alone: the spiritual world withdrew. Human beings now had to create a culture *from below upwards.*

This was expressed in Mesopotamia by building stepped towers and temple towers: ziggurats. A longing set in directed upwards, towards heaven. What is interpreted by the Bible as pride: 'let us build ... a tower with its top in the heavens' (Gen.11:4) can also be seen as mankind's longing to be close to the gods.

This was also the time when the Egyptian pyramids were built. The Greek historian Herodotus pointed out the polarity between the Egyptian pyramids and the Babylonian temple towers, the ziggurats.

The Egyptian pyramids gave the impression of having been built *from above downwards.* Their form follows heavenly proportions. They are monuments to the dead for the souls who are in the spiritual world. The pyramid graves depict the journey of the soul living in the spiritual world. In the pyramids it is as though heaven is brought down to earth.

In contrast, the Babylonian ziggurats are enormous towers. Like stairs to heaven the giant flights of steps lead to the high terrace which is a place of cult worship. It is as though the towers strive towards the heights in order to follow the lost heaven, the lost gods.

From the stepped towers the priests watched for sky phenomena and movements of the stars.

The interpretation of omens

Mesopotamia was really an ideal region for observing the stars: no rain for half the year, a permanently clear sky, no clouds, sun every day and an incomparably beautiful starry sky at night. Human beings in the land of the two rivers felt the power of the skies deeply. This sky made a huge impression on people's souls at that time: it was divine. Anu, the power of heaven, was felt to be a godlike being.

The sky phenomena which shone most brightly — Sun, Moon and Venus — were of the greatest importance to the Mesopotamians. They formed the divine triad, the trinity. They were carefully observed from the temple towers.

The gods revealed themselves in the stars and planets. The planets as such were not viewed as deities, but as places where the gods who were concealed behind them appeared. As interpreters, the planets intimated the will of the gods to men. The Sun was where the Sun god Utu appeared (Shamash in the later Akkadian language), the Moon was the manifestation of Nanna (Akkadian: Suen) and Venus was the manifestation of Inanna (Akkadian: Ishtar).

These three heavenly bodies (Sun Moon and Venus) were accurately observed even in the most ancient times (before 1700 BC), because they were important messengers of the gods. The priests turned their gaze to the stars and felt that, 'there the gods make themselves known.' Human beings tried to read the will of the gods in the stars. This led to the development of a star wisdom which was also a religion.

The special nature of this star wisdom was that the sky phenomena were an omen. Everything that happened in the skies had its counterpart in events taking place at the same time on earth. It was felt that the phenomena in the starry sky displayed a rhythm, a regularity. Any deviation from this regularity was viewed as ominous. It was an omen, a portent.

Many omen texts have been handed down to us from this period. One example:

> In the month of Abu on the sixth day Nin-dar-anna appears [this is Venus 'the bright ruler of the sky'] in the east; rains will be in the heavens, there will be devastations. Until the tenth day of Nisannu she stands in the east; at the eleventh day she disappears ... on the eleventh day of Duzu Nin-dar-anna flares up in the west. Hostility will be in the land; the crops will prosper.'[1]

These are observations of Nin-dar-anna, Venus, which are seen as omens, as portents.

The interpretation of omens applied to two areas. On the one hand to weather, to floods, droughts, natural catastrophes, harvest predictions, etc. (rains will be in the heavens, the crops will prosper). On the other hand to political events, to the fate of the land or the people, to the course of wars, etc. (hostility will be in the land). Eclipses were also viewed as portents:

> If an eclipse of the Moon occurs on the fifteenth, then the son of the king will kill his father and take possession of the throne or an enemy will rise up and devour the land. If the eclipse occurs on the twenty-first, then rain will be hindered in the sky and high water in the springs.

Meteorological phenomena were also seen as portents:

> If the Moon is surrounded by a halo and if the ascending Jupiter stands inside this, then the king of Amurru will become powerful and slay the enemy.[2]

The formation of clouds and halos, the brightness and colour of the stars were thus also taken into account when making interpretations.

Portents were of the greatest importance for people of that time, because they expressed something about the invisible powers which were all around. It was possible to obtain knowledge of the intentions of these powers through omens and to try to gain their favour. Although the gods revealed their intentions in the form of signs, human beings could nevertheless always do something to avert or influence an anticipated disaster. The idea of an unalterable or inevitable fate in the stars was totally alien to the people of that time.

In myth

In Mesopotamia the interpretation of omens was inseparably connected to its culture. The development of portents even played an important role in the creation myths of this people. The god Enki, the lord of the earth, was the central figure in the creation events and was revered as an oracle and as the god of wisdom.

It was no easy task for the gods to create the world: to begin with the gods groaned under the burden of their divine tasks. Enki's mother Nammu (the goddess who had given birth to heaven and earth) sought the advice of her son. Enki came up with the solution. He advised his mother to produce creatures who would help the gods with their work, in other words, assistants in the work of creation. The creation of mankind then began and, after many dramatic events and complications, human beings were indeed created.

But people also needed to have a destiny. How was this to be arranged? Nammu (Enki's mother, the archetypal mother *per se)* was allotted the difficult task of determining a destiny for human beings. People now wanted to be able to see into the future, an understandable wish. They wanted to find out what the gods were up to. Who was better suited to fulfil this justified wish of human beings than Enki whose idea it had been to create humankind? So Enki created a system of portents which should enable human beings to study the will of the gods. But people should not be able to find out about their destiny without some effort. So Enki created a system of portents which left nothing to be desired as regards divine refinement in its mysteriousness and ambiguity. Mankind could now study the will of the gods, but at the same time this paved the way for a wealth of superstition as well as fear of bad omens, forebodings of evil, illusionary dreams, etc.

Enki was always fond of human beings and well disposed towards them. He mediated between gods and men by disclosing the will of the gods to them through innumerable signs. However, this will of the gods was never imperative nor inevitable. People were always able to do something in order to change the course of events and avoid potential disaster. Thus it was Enki who gave the sign to Utnapishtim when the gods later decided to destroy mankind in a flood. Enki's warning portent told Utnapishtim (the Mesopotamian Noah) to build an ark so that mankind could survive the flood.

Characteristics of the portents

The following features characterize the interpretation of omens at that time:

First, amongst the sky phenomena it was the movements and the way in which the Sun, Moon and planets appeared which were seen as omens. Omens never included any reference to the zodiac. The zodiac as a unity of twelve constellations was unknown at the time. The planetary positions in the constellations were of no importance at all. Only rising, setting, movements and visibility were of significance.

Secondly, the omens were universal in nature. As already mentioned, they were related to:

— the general political circumstances of the country and the people;
— nature: the weather, harvest prospects, natural catastrophes, etc.

Individual human destiny was not considered at this point.

Thirdly, the portents were not read from people's birth constellations. Astrology associated with an individual's birth did not exist at that date. Only the phenomena present in the sky at a particular moment were viewed as portents.

Fourthly, the gods announced their intentions through omens

in the sky. The signs given by the gods were never imperative: their aim was to show people their task. The threat of disaster could be avoided or prevented by sacrifice, rituals of atonement, etc. As already stated, the idea of an unalterable fate in the stars was utterly alien to the people of that time.

4. The Dark Age

Great changes took place in Mesopotamia around 1400 BC. The ancient Babylonian civilization collapsed due to invasion by the Hittites (around 1530 BC). Two centuries later a new civilization arose in the land of the two rivers with Assur as its capital: the Assyrian civilization which, after only a few centuries, was to dominate the whole of Mesopotamia.

This civilization had a very different character to the Babylonian one. The Assyrians were true fighters. They appeared to have been made for the role of warriors. They are depicted sitting in their chariots with muscular bodies and impressive decorations in hair and beard. They conquered the whole of Mesopotamia, Syria and large parts of Asia Minor in the centuries after 1350 BC. They were infamous for their brutal abduction of whole tribes and were feared because they showed no pity for their conquered foes. The Assyrian empire only collapsed around 614 BC.

A great deal has been learned about this culture from the library which King Ashurbanipal assembled in his palace. This, the oldest library in the world (25000 clay tablets), was excavated in Nineveh in 1850. Ashurbanipal was a keen supporter of art and science. He tracked down old texts in all the towns and temples in his empire. These he collected, had copied and the copies stored systematically. These texts give us a picture of the customs and viewpoints of the time, religion, culture and social relationships.

Great importance was attached to the sky phenomena for life on earth, as is proved by 4,000 clay tablets in the collection of omens belonging to king Ashurbanipal. Not only the Sun, Moon and Venus, but also Saturn, Jupiter, Mars and Mercury were seen as messengers of the gods. The interpretation of omens had a universal character, for instance:

> When, with the light of her fire, Venus illuminates the heart of the Scorpion whose tail is dark and whose horns shine brightly, then rain and flood will devastate the land. Locusts will come and lay waste to the land. Oxen and cattle will be decimated.
>
> If Jupiter is in front of the Moon, then a great king will die, but if it is behind the Moon, then there will be hostilities in our own land. If Jupiter stands at the right horn of the Moon, then the king of Akkad will die, if it stands at the left horn, then the kind of Amurru will die.[1]

However, the Assyrians' star religion had a very different character to the earlier ancient Babylonian one. Although the Assyrian priests also practised an astrology of omens, the character of the omens had changed. They no longer left people free as previously, but took on an authoritative character, giving expression to an unbending will of the gods. The events foretold by the omens could no longer be prevented.

Accordingly, the Assyrian religion was characterized by powerful gods who were both honoured and feared because they determined fate and demanded obedience. Human beings had scarcely any influence to change what the gods wanted. The Assyrians were not filled with trust in the goodness of their gods, but with the fear of not satisfying the demands made by the gods concerning ritual and conduct.

The consciousness of sin was highly developed. The attempt was made to win the favour of the gods and appease their wrath through prayers, sacrifices, rites of atonement, etc. After death the human being ended up in 'the land from which there is no return,' in the shadows of the underworld. The Assyrian's world view had a pessimistic note with no prospect of a light-filled life after death and no hope of salvation from earthly suffering. They attempted to protect themselves from the threatening disaster.

The religion of the Assyrians was closely connected with magic, divination (fortune telling) and the interpretation of omens. The clay tablets from King Ashurbanipal's library show that the priests collected enormous quantities of omens of all kinds to find out about the will of the gods. The omens of greatest importance were those found by hepatoscopy — reading the liver of sacrificed animals. Just as the lines on human hands differ, so no two sheep livers are the same. The gods made known their will in these differences.

Oil divination, in which oil was poured into water and the movements and forms of the oil drops interpreted, was also popular. The interpretation of the flickering of a flame, the behaviour of animals (snakes, ants, dogs, sheep, etc.), the flight of birds and the meaning of dreams were developed into a comprehensive science. The omens in sky phenomena only formed a small part of a multitude of omens during that period.

These omens were used by the priests to study the will of the gods, so that offences against divine predestination could be avoided.

Numerous exorcism texts bear witness to the fact that the priests also had the task of appeasing the enraged gods. For the Assyrians, the omens were no longer revelatory signs from kindly disposed gods as before, but the expression of forceful demands and decisions of fate from powerful gods. The interpretations were predictions which would inevitably come to pass. Astrologers whose predictions and prophecies were not fulfilled were severely punished.

What might happen if the predictions of the interpreter of omens did not come true is illustrated in a letter. The king's omen interpreter had interpreted an eclipse of the Sun as a bad portent for the country. After this unfavourable prediction had not come true, he wrote the following letter to his king:

> To the king of countries ... An eclipse has happened but it was not visible in the capital. As that eclipse approached, at the capital where the king dwells, behold the clouds were everywhere, and whether the eclipse took place or did not take place we don't know ...
>
> The great gods who dwell in the city of the king, my lord, overcast the sky and did not permit to see the eclipse. So let the king know that this eclipse was not directed at the king, my lord, nor his land.[2]

In this instance, the protective gods had covered the city with a layer of cloud to show that the omen should not come into effect. The interpreter of omens could not know this in advance of course.

The changing character of omens

It is clear that in Assyria the astrology of omens gradually took on a form in which the omens lost their earlier liberal character and were increasingly taken as the expression of inescapable conditions. To what degree this was already so in the ancient Babylonian culture has not been determined with certainty due to the difficulty of dating the surviving omen texts accurately. What is certain, however, is that at the time of King Ashurbanipal, the omens were still of a universal nature. They were related to the fate of the country and the people, to succession, wars, natural catastrophes, harvests, etc. There was not a single omen in the king's library which referred to the personal destiny of one human being. Individual birth horoscopy only emerged later.

The transition from liberal to compelling omens was therefore related to universal omens at first. What was the cause of this transition?

The dark age in which human beings increasingly became citizens of the earth progressed. From having lived amongst spiritual beings, the human being became fully incarnated on the earth and his soul became increasingly connected to the body.

The fact that the ability to see into the spiritual world was lost to mankind to an increasing degree from the beginning of the dark age was due to the human soul becoming more and more connected to and dependent on the physical body.

This attachment of the soul to the physical body had to take place to an increasing degree after the Fall. This had very significant consequences for the relationship of the human being to the cosmos because mankind's physical structure developed from the cosmos.

In the world of the stars before birth, the human being along with the beings of the hierarchies prepares his body for the coming life on earth. In the world of the stars a spiritual seed is worked on over long periods of time. All the cosmic qualities are worked into the spiritual form of this physical body. The joining of the spiritual seed and the physical seed enable the development of the human organism.

Because the human form is born from the cosmos it has a relationship to it — it is a reflection of the macrocosm. Think for example of the pictures of the 'zodiac man' handed down from earlier centuries which show how the human form is connected to the zodiac: Aries (the head), Taurus (the larynx), Gemini (the arms), etc.

Until a few hundred years ago human beings were familiar with the idea that the human form was connected to the spiritual powers of the cosmos on account of these traditional images. But it is wrong to think of matter in this context. Essentially the physical body is not matter. The *matter* of our physical body is replaced, but the *form* of the physical body is connected to cosmic forces and remains throughout life. Our organs are connected to the planets, to the planetary processes.

Sun: heart
Saturn: spleen
Jupiter: liver
Mars: gall bladder
Venus: kidneys
Mercury: lungs
Moon: reproductive organs

These relationships refer to organic *processes.*

The cosmos is therefore within us, in our body. It is often said that 'the human being is a microcosm related to the macrocosm.' This is due to the fact that the whole macrocosm lives in a contracted, concentrated form in our body. Our 'bodily cosmos' arose after a long preparation before birth in the world of the stars. What lives in our bodily cosmos during life on earth is a consequence of prebirth conditions, it is the *ongoing effects of the past* from the heavenly cosmos.

When the human being connects to the physical body at birth he also makes a connection to what was worked into this body in the prebirth world of the stars. This is expressed in the birth constellation. At birth the human being is assigned a particular constellation which expresses those powers which have led him into physical existence.[3]

At the dawn of the dark age, dependency on the physical body *had* to increase. The ever stronger attachment of the soul to the body during the dark age is a consequence of the Fall.

Originally the human being was in paradise where he lived as a heavenly being among celestial beings. It was only through the Fall that a growing attachment took place of the spiritual and emotional — and hence also of human destiny — to the physical.

Human destiny was increasingly determined by what had been worked into the body before birth. A growing dependency appeared on what was expressed by the birth constellation.

In the course of the dark age the possibility gradually arose for what we nowadays know as birth horoscopy. As we shall see (in Chapters 6 and 7), it was only after the time of Christ, however, that working with birth constellations of individual human beings emerged. The slowly emerging attachment of the soul to the body became noticeable long before that. It helped to emphasize the negative aspects in the interpretation of omens. The omens were increasingly taken as the expression of a relationship to the spiritual world which could not be influenced. Human consciousness was less and less able to reach into the world of the gods. Total uncertainty spread about the reasons for the gods commanding or deciding one thing rather than another. The gods responsible for determining fate were themselves hidden from the Assyrians, completely beyond reach. Only their actions, their interception in destiny, could be felt.

As the dark age progressed, human beings felt that their fate was determined by unknown spiritual powers and that the world of the gods could scarcely be reached by human consciousness any more. The twilight of the gods was evident in experiences of this kind.

The tragic mood of the twilight of the gods in Assyria is expressed more clearly in the following disconsolate prayer than in any description:

> May the god whom I do not know be calmed, may the goddess whom I do not know be calmed ... Goddess whom I know or do not know, the sins are grave, the omissions are grave. I know not the omissions which I have committed ... I constantly look for help — no one reaches a hand out to me ... The people are deaf, they know not ... whether they trespass or whether they do right.[4]

5. The Fate of the Star Mysteries

During the third post-Atlantean cultural epoch star wisdom experienced a great flowering in the mysteries. The fate of star wisdom was deeply connected to what took place in the mystery centres. As the clairvoyant faculties were progressively lost with the onset of the dark age (around 3100 BC), the mysteries became of increasing importance for the development of culture. At that time the mysteries were centres of education which attempted to maintain a connection to the spiritual world. Pupils were shown ways by which the soul could be freed from its attachment to the body. The consequences of the Fall were reversed, even though this might only be for a few moments. The soul could thus be led back into the old way of seeing. As a preparation for initiation the pupils had to pass difficult tests which gave them deep insights into the evolution of the earth and of mankind. The pupils came to know spiritual realities so deeply that afterwards they were totally transformed human beings. It was as though they had passed through death and awoken to a higher life. This prepared them for taking on particular tasks in the guidance of mankind.

A veil of secrecy always surrounded the mysteries. The initiation methods remained secret as they could lead to dangerous misuse in the hands of the inexperienced. Misuse of this kind had, for example, led to the sinking of Atlantis in ancient times.[1]

Due to this secrecy, nothing has been passed down to us of what happened in the star mysteries in the Egyptian-Babylonian-Chaldean epoch. The Greek historian Herodotus who had visited Egypt, mentioned several times in his account of the journey that he had to remain silent on certain matters.

Nowadays, in the age of the consciousness soul, our situation is very different in this respect. We are so secure in our ego consciousness that we are able to carry the moral responsibility for our own actions. Rudolf Steiner was therefore able to make public the conditions and methods for a possible modern initiation path.[2] He was also able to describe in full the initiation procedures of the earlier mysteries. His accounts show that the initiation methods used by different peoples were entirely different. The methods were also modified over the course of time as human nature changed. However, what the mysteries had in common was that means were sought to achieve initiation in order to free the soul at least temporarily from the increasingly strong attachment to the physical body.

However, what took place in the mysteries was only open to a small group of chosen pupils, to an elite as it were. The larger part of humanity became increasingly attached to the physical body. In the mystery centres the soul's release from the body was only possible for a limited period of time, and so the consequences of the Fall could only be reversed temporarily.

There were two aspects to what took place in the mysteries. On the one hand the path followed by the mysteries had a *retrograde* orientation. It tried to reproduce past states of consciousness, to reawaken the old way of seeing. However, what took place in the mysteries also worked as a *preparation* for the future. The pupil of the mysteries was lead to an out-of-body experience of the spiritual being who would one day descend to the earth to save mankind from the consequences of the Fall. This sun being, the approaching Christ, could be experienced in the mysteries. This had already been prophesied in the pre-Christian mysteries.

The decline of the Egyptian star mysteries

The advancement of the dark age also had an impact on the mysteries. Even for initiates it became more difficult to reach the highest spiritual realms. At that time in Egypt, around 1300 BC, a decisive transformation took place in the mysteries: the star wisdom was felt to be fading more and more. The star goddess

Isis, who could still be perceived in the oldest mysteries, not only remained mute but she became powerlessness.

Rudolf Steiner described what a pupil of the oldest Egyptian star mysteries went through in his initiation. After being appropriately prepared and tested, the pupil could be led into the higher worlds. He experienced being raised into sublime spiritual realms. There he came to know those spiritual beings who created mankind's physical and etheric bodies. After having experienced this, the pupil could enter a lofty spiritual region, a sacred place where he felt connected to the power of the stars. He came to know the being working on mankind's innermost astral being. He experienced this not as the working of powers, but as a motherly being of the earth: Isis herself. The pupil felt himself connected to her and experienced how she awakened in him a deep longing for self-knowledge. Looking at her he felt the question: what is the innermost being of man? This question lay heavy on the heart of the pupil. But Isis gave no answer, remaining mute and silent.

Because the pupil's longing for an answer to this question continued to flow into Isis, the mother of the earth, after some time she gave birth to another being, Osiris. Osiris was the creative sounding word of worlds. This resounded inwardly in the pupil's soul. The experience of Osiris was the solution to the innermost riddle of mankind for him. Hearing the word of worlds, in initiation he became one with Isis and the word of worlds born out of her. This made it possible for him to know himself as a human being in the deeper sense. He attained self-knowledge of his eternal being.

Initiation could only be undergone in this form up to the time of Moses. From then on the lofty goddess of the stars was powerless to give birth to the word of worlds. Although she was still experienced in the mysteries she was the powerless Isis who could no longer lead to the experience of the word of worlds. From that time onwards the star mysteries lacked a living spiritual content. Those who rose to higher worlds through the mysteries felt themselves lonely and abandoned because Osiris, the word of worlds, could no longer be experienced. The fact was that the divine was losing its power in the spiritual realms. The divine god was about to leave the worlds where he had previously been experienced. In the later Egyptian period when an initiate looked into the spiritual worlds he shared in the death of god in the spiritual world.

Rudolf Steiner described it in the following way:

> And ever more and more did this feeling condense itself into what one may call the supersensible equivalent of that which one encounters in the sense-world as the death of man — when one sees a person die, when one knows that he is passing out of the physical world. And now, when the initiate of the later Egyptian age rose up into the higher worlds, he was a partaker in the gradual dying of the god. As one feels with a person when he is passing into the spiritual world, so did the initiate of the later Egyptian period feel how the god took leave of the spiritual world in order to pass over into another world. This was the significant and remarkable part of the later Egyptian initiation — that when the aspirant raised his life into the spiritual worlds, it was not into rapture and bliss, but in order to partake in the gradual passing away of a god who was present in these higher worlds as cosmic word and cosmic harmony.[3]

The mood of initiates of the late Egyptian period was therefore one of sorrow and resignation. Their souls felt the deepest sorrow for the death of god in the spiritual world. But this sorrow was mixed with a slight hope: where is god now? In which sphere should we seek him? Perhaps he is now coming to us on the earth. Perhaps he is closer to us as earthly human beings than he was before.[4]

The time around 1300 BC therefore heralded the decline of the living star wisdom and the rise of the anticipation of a Saviour, the hope of the coming of Christ, the hope of a saviour who would redeem mankind from the consequences of the Fall.

A turning point in the history of the world

The timing of the transition around 1300 BC is connected with the Sothic cycle which is of such importance for the wisdom of the stars. As described in Chapter 2, each of these cycles was characterized by the fact that the power of clairvoyance declined by a further step. The original highest and cosmically all-encompassing clairvoyance gradually darkened.

It is no coincidence that the flowering of Egyptian culture in which star wisdom was still alive coincided exactly with the Sothic cycle from about 2780 to 1320 BC. The next Sothic cycle, lasting from about 1320 BC to AD 140, was the period when living wisdom of the stars died away.[5]

We shall briefly summarize Rudolf Steiner's observations on this important turning point. Like every cultural epoch, the Egyptian culture had an important task in the whole evolution of mankind. It had a lofty mission which it was able to accomplish on the basis of the old clairvoyant consciousness. However, the overall evolution of mankind progresses in such a way that a mission of this kind is allocated a certain period of time. Time can run out for the mission in question and this was the case for the mission of the Egyptian people in the time of Moses around 1300 BC.

Mankind was to be called upon to develop those powers of the soul which were to replace the old dim clairvoyance. Self-consciousness, intellectuality, reason and judgment were to enter mankind in place of the old clairvoyance. This new element had to grow out of the Egyptian one, but the Egyptian people were not able to realize this task themselves. Starting from the Egyptian culture, Moses' task was to bring about a change of direction and bridge the gulf between the old and new times.

It is not without reason that many artists — Michelangelo being the greatest of these — have portrayed Moses with ram's horns on his forehead as a symbol of self-aware thinking. Moses had the proclivity for intellectuality, but intellectual thinking arose in the old clairvoyant way in him. He was unable to develop the power of reason out of a fully awake self-consciousness as mankind could do later. In Moses the proclivity towards intellectuality appeared for the first time within clairvoyance. This was precisely the reason why he was able to create the transition to the next cultural epoch.

Moses was brought up in Egypt at the court of the Pharaoh (Exod.2:2). He was initiated into the Egyptian mysteries. 'And Moses was instructed in all the wisdom of the Egyptians, and he was mighty in his words and deeds.' (Acts 7:22). Moses was not only initiated in the mysteries of Egypt, he also took them with him. At the time when he led his people out of Egypt he knew the secret of the word of worlds as it lived in the Egyptian mysteries. He knew that it was no longer possible to experience the word of worlds in the spiritual worlds and that it was preparing to become active in earthly spheres. This allowed him to sense Christ's approach to the earth in what was announced in the burning bush and in the fire on Sinai. Moses had the task of creating the transition from the Egyptian culture to the next epoch.[6]

6. The Hebrew People: Preparation for the Turning Point of Time

The history of the Hebrews shows a pendulum movement between the two parallel cultures of the third post-Atlantean cultural epoch, Mesopotamia and Egypt.

Abraham was born (around 2000 BC) in 'Ur in Chaldea' (Gen.11:31), that is, in Mesopotamia. He grew up in the land of the two rivers and then moved to Haran in the north of the country. Haran was famous at the time for the temple of the Moon god whose culture dominated the whole of Mesopotamia. The Bible therefore calls the land of the two rivers Shinar (Gen.10:10) after the Moon god Sin. Haran was the centre of the Moon mysteries and the site where the star mysteries were kept. It was there that Abraham acquired the star wisdom of Mesopotamia.

In Haran God called on Abraham to leave his homeland: 'Go from your country and your kindred and your father's house to the land that I will show you' (Gen.12:1). Abraham was led to Canaan and from there to Egypt where he mixed with the initiated rulers.

Legend tells that there Abraham 'became wiser than all men before him' because he learned arithmetic and the lore of the stars from the Egyptian sages.[1] Only after Abraham had assimilated the Egyptian mysteries was he able to begin his real task in Canaan, in the middle between Egypt and Mesopotamia. The area between the Jordan and the Mediterranean coast was called Canaan in ancient times, and later became the 'promised land' of the Bible (Num.34).

With Abraham the pendulum movement of the Hebrew people between Mesopotamia and Egypt began. This continued throughout the entire further history of this people.

The Bible tells how Abraham was determined to prevent his son Isaac, who had been born in Canaan, from taking a woman 'from the daughters of the Canaanites' (Gen.24:3). His wife was to be brought from Mesopotamia, from the city of Nahor. It is assumed that this refers to the city where his uncle Nahor lived, in other words the temple city of Haran where the Babylonian star mysteries flourished. The Bible clearly points out that the Hebrews were to be strongly influenced by the Babylonian star mysteries.

Isaac's son, Jacob, was also sent from Canaan to Mesopotamia by his father in order to find his wife there. Jacob remained there for twenty years before returning to Canaan. This resulted in eleven of his twelve sons being born in Mesopotamia and only the youngest, Benjamin, being born after his return to Canaan. Jacob wrestled with the angel who gave him a new name: Israel (Gen.32:29). This became the name of the people descended from him. Jacob spent the last seventeen years of his life not in Canaan but in Egypt where he died.

Joseph, Jacob's son, was born in Babylonia. However, his destiny was fulfilled in Egypt where he was initiated into the mysteries and as viceroy led the country through difficult times. Joseph's eleven brothers followed him to Egypt. So the people of Israel grew up in Egypt and in its culture for four centuries. Only when they began to suffer oppression did Moses lead them out of Egypt back to the 'promised land.'

Much later, in the sixth century BC the pendulum swung the other way again. The years of captivity in Babylonia are also part of the history of this people.

A link between two cultures

What is behind the deep involvement of the Hebrew people with the cultures of Egypt and Mesopotamia?

The third cultural epoch had a remarkable double nature, flowering both along the Nile and in Mesopotamia. The unusual aspect of this double nature will become clear when we consider the inner character of both cultures.

The Babylonian culture was focussed *outwards.* It sought for the spirit in the outer world, in nature, in the world of the senses. The search for the spirit took place in the world of space.

The Egyptian culture sought a way *inwards,* to a spiritual world which cannot be found in the world of the senses but in the life between death and a new birth. The spirit was sought in the stream of time.

These two cultures therefore strove for two paths to the spirit with opposite directions.

Both the Egyptian and the Babylonian cultures were great in themselves, but neither was in a position to give birth to the seed of what needed to come about in the future. Further development required cross-fertilization between the two cultures. Because these cultures followed opposite paths, this cross-fertilization could not take place directly but required the creation of a linking element.

Rudolf Steiner described how the Hebrew people had the task of forming this link.[2] It originated in Ur in Chaldea and in Haran assimilated the revelations which come from outside. Then it went to Egypt where it came to know the Egyptian mysteries and assimilated that which comes from inside. The purpose of this involvement with the two neighbouring cultures was to assimilate the mystery impulses which they carried.

It may appear contradictory that the mystery impulses of these cultures where a star wisdom flourished were taken up by the Hebrew people, who totally rejected any guidance from the stars. What is the meaning of this mysterious contradiction?

Rudolf Steiner was able to shed light on the Hebrew people's extraordinary relationship to the world of the stars.[3] This extraordinary relationship was connected to the special task they had, which was to prepare the physical body that would be a vessel for the being of Christ. This preparation began with the pact which Abraham made with God, and worked through the blood, through heredity and through the course of generations until the birth of Jesus of Nazareth. Due to this pact with Yahweh the Hebrew people had a different physical constitution and a different relationship to the world of stars than the neighbouring peoples had.

Abraham was promised a son with the prophesy, 'I will surely multiply your offspring as the stars of heaven' (Gen.22:17). A more appropriate translation would be: 'Your offspring will be ordered as the stars in the heavens,' because we find:

> images of the twelve signs of the zodiac in the twelve sons of Jacob, in the twelve tribes of the Israelites. As the speech of the gods was expressed above in the twelve constellations of the zodiac, so Yahweh expressed himself through the blood flowing through the generations of the Hebrew people which divided into the twelve tribes from the twelve sons of Jacob.[4]

The Hebrew people differed from their neighbours because the powers of the stars were imprinted in them through the blood flowing down the generations. The neighbouring peoples possessed clairvoyant faculties for the world of the stars. Although these were already becoming decadent in the second millennium before Christ there was still an echo of being able to see the star gods. The Babylonians worshipped:

the Sun god: Shamash
the Moon god: Sin
the Venus god: Ishtar
the Mercury god: Nabu
the Mars god: Nergal
the Jupiter god: Marduk
the Saturn god: Ninurte, etc.

The powers of the soul available to the neighbouring peoples for clairvoyance were active in a different manner in the Hebrew people. They turned inwards causing a transformation of the bodily constitution.

The same powers which enabled clairvoyance in other peoples were active in such a way in the Hebrew people that they transformed their physical nature and made it more perfect. The working of Yahweh increased the perfection of the physical body.

Because Yahweh was active in forming the physical body, people's consciousness of god was turned inwards. What other peoples beheld in the widths of space, in the world of the stars, turned to inner consciousness in the Hebrew people. Yahweh was the invisible God who never revealed himself in the celestial phenomena. Because God did not reveal his will through the stars, the Hebrew people had to develop a totally different relationship to the world of the stars than that of other peoples. Although the existence of the star and planetary gods was not denied, no one was allowed to turn to these beings. The worship of Yahweh was incompatible with the worship of the gods of stars and planets.

Due to this form of monotheism, the Hebrew people were quite different to all the peoples around them who had developed a wisdom of the stars. Star wisdom was always connected to the worship of many gods. The Israelite's task consisted in raising themselves above these star gods; for this they had to reject the multiplicity of gods. Through monotheism their consciousness was guided to the coming Christ, to the Saviour.

Warnings against guidance from the stars

This explains why the Old Testament so often warns against guidance from the stars.

The being of Christ redeems the consequences of the Fall for mankind. This enables mankind to overcome their dependency on the world of the stars. In preparation for this, the individual of the Israelites needed to raise himself above the power of fate of the stars. Interpretation of the stars was firmly rejected. They had to turn to Yahweh who was higher than the gods of the stars.

If there were heavenly powers which revealed themselves in the stars and planets, then these could only be lower beings than 'the Lord of Hosts' himself. Any turning towards these lower beings would be disobeying and falling away from the God of

Israel. Belief in the power of the stars would deeply offend the supreme majesty and uniqueness of Yahweh who transcended the whole visible world.

The Old Testament repeatedly warns about the star cults of the surrounding peoples.

> Therefore take good heed to yourselves ... lest you act corruptly by making a graven image for yourselves ... And beware lest you lift up your eyes to heaven, and when you see the Sun and the Moon and the stars, all the host of heaven, you be drawn away and worship them and serve them. (Deut.4:15–19)
>
> If there is found among you, within any of your towns ... a man or woman who ... has gone and served other gods and worshipped them, or the Sun or the Moon or any of the host of heaven ... then you shall bring forth to your gates that man or woman ... and you shall stone that man or woman to death with stones.' (Deut.17:2–5)
>
> There shall not be found among you any one who ... practices divination, a soothsayer ... For whoever does these things is an abomination to the Lord.' (Deut.18:10–12)

It is repeatedly stated that no one shall bow before the celestial bodies, subjugate themselves to the stars or serve idols. These warnings were necessary because the people of the Old Testament were surrounded by peoples who were involved with star wisdom and the interpretation of omens.

Most of the warnings are given in Deuteronomy, the fifth book of the Bible, which begins as follows: 'These are the words that Moses spoke to all Israel ...' The warnings date from the time of Moses (*c.* 1300 BC); as mentioned in relation to the Sothic cycles, this period formed a decisive turning point in the history of the wisdom of the stars.

7. The Emergence of the Birth Horoscope

The oldest recorded birth planetary aspects for a person date from 410 BC from Babylon. There it says, 'in the night of the fourteenth of the month ... a son of Shuma Ushur was born' and that at this time 'the Moon stood above the horn of Scorpio, Jupiter in Pisces, Venus in Taurus, Saturn in Cancer and Mars in Gemini.' It is also noted that Mercury was not visible.[1]

It is noticeable that the exact *hour* of birth is not yet taken into account. There is no mention of which planets are above the horizon and which are below. Only the locations of the Moon and planets on the *day* of birth are indicated and this in a very general way.

This birth aspect is not yet a 'horoscope,' because the term 'horoscope' is derived from the Greek *horoskopos,* that is, observation of time. Originally it was only called a horoscope if the exact hour of birth, that is, the rising sign on the eastern horizon, the ascendent was defined.

The next record of birth aspects dates from 263 BC, in other words, from ancient Greek times. This gives the positions of the Sun and Moon in the zodiac very precisely: 'The Sun was at 13°30' in Aries, the Moon at 10° in Aquarius, Jupiter at the beginning of Leo, Venus and Mercury were with the Sun [that is, in the same sign], Saturn and Mars in Cancer.' The remainder of the text is incomplete. It is nevertheless possible to recognize the way in which the stars were interpreted at that time. The text continues as follows: 'He will lack prosperity ... his food will not be able to satisfy his hunger. The wealth which he posed in youth will be lacking in old age. His days will appear long to him. His wife, who will be seduced by others in his absence, ... He will have ...'[2] This is another birth constellation *without* information on the exact hour of birth.

The first record of a birth horoscope in the real sense, with details of the exact time of birth, is not from Mesopotamia but from Greece and dates from 70 BC. Birth horoscopes were therefore only developed about two thousand years ago.

What prompted this development?

Advances in astronomical knowledge at the time enabled planetary positions and aspects to be identified with ever greater precision. This may have contributed to the development of individual astrology. However, the most important factor was the growing interest in human beings as individuals. In earlier cultures the individual was of little importance: only the fate of society and the state mattered and therefore the interpretation of the stars was wholly devoted to these entities.

This was still the case in the Chaldean empire. It was founded in 626 BC by Nabopolassar and lasted until it was overthrown by the Persians in 539 BC. In the Chaldean empire the powerful priest class exercised great influence over matters of state. The Chaldean priests made careful observations of the course of the Sun, the movements of the planets and the Moon, eclipses of the Sun and Moon, and so on. They used what they read in the stars to advise whoever was in power. The fame of these Chaldean temple astrologers was so great that they were viewed as ideal teachers of star lore for many centuries. They did not practise any individual astrology, but worked solely in the service of general matters of politics, the state and the people. Their knowledge was also used in the founding of cities. Laying the foundation stone at a favourable cosmic time guaranteed the successful development of the city and the prosperity of its inhabitants.

Interest in individual human beings arose gradually with the development of the intellectual or mind soul, that is, after the eighth century BC. It is only the advancing individualization which accompanied this development of the soul which can account for the emergence of individual birth horoscopy in the final centuries before Christ.

It is notable that astrological activity itself became independent of the collective context at the same time. Astrologers working individually began to appear. Up until the seventh century BC, interpretation of star constellations was a matter for the mystery centres. It was practised by priests of the mysteries. Charged with interpreting the stars they had religious duties to fulfil in addition to their astrological tasks. The library of King Ashurbanipal contains the names of individual astrologers, such as Akkullanu and Balasi. These very first astrologers whom we know by name were advisors to King Esarhaddon, Ashurbanipal's predecessor. These astrologers were priests and worked in the service of the Temple of Ea (also called Enki), the god of wisdom and the oracle.

After about 600 BC, astrological activity began to be emancipated from its association with the mysteries. The first wandering astrologers appeared in Chaldea. They were pupils of the Chaldean temple guardians who were still viewed as the only ones initiated into the ancient wisdom of the stars. In later centuries they moved to Greece where, due to the great fame of the Chaldean star wisdom, they were known everywhere as 'Chaldeans.' Due to their activity, the name 'Chaldean' was adopted as a synonym for *all* astrologers in ancient times, even when they were natives and had nothing to do with Chaldea. The prophet Daniel (sixth century BC) thus spoke of astrology as the 'language of the Chaldeans' (Dan.1:4).

The interest in the birth constellations of individual people arose gradually in Chaldea in the final centuries before Christ. But the birth horoscope first came to full flower on Greek soil.

It is extraordinary how quickly a system for interpreting birth horoscopes was developed in Ancient Greece. It only took two centuries (by around AD 150) to develop the elements of birth horoscopy which are still used to this day. For example:

1. calculating birth constellations which take account of the exact time and place of birth;
2. dividing the space into what is known as the twelve houses or fields which are related to the horizon and are believed to be meaningful for specific areas of life;
3. the theory of aspects which attaches importance to the

relationships of the angles between the position of the planets in the horoscope (conjunction, square, trine, opposition);

4. working with zodiac signs rather than constellations, that is with twelve equal signs of 30°, calculated from the spring equinox.

This development took place astonishingly quickly, as Ptolemy wrote his comprehensive astrological treatise, the *Tetrabiblos* or Four Books, between AD 140 and 150. This became a standard work which was to become the astrologers' bible for the next 1500 years. It summarized (exactly at the end of the Sothic cycle) the body of developed knowledge so well that it was almost impossible to add anything fundamentally new for many hundreds of years. The Tetrabiblos was responsible for defining the further development of astrology.

Even the fact that Ptolemy replaced the sidereal zodiac (the constellations) with the tropical zodiac (beginning with the spring equinox) had a decisive influence on the astrology which followed. Since then astrologers use 30° sections of the signs rather than constellations.

Planetary tables and ephemerides existed, so that it was possible to calculate horoscopes without ever having looked at the sky, without a single upward glance. What had originally been reverential and wondering observation of the heavens, the world of the gods, now became a matter of calculation and interpretation which everyone could do at home in their own room.

How was this development in astrology set in motion in Greek culture? What was the stimulus for it? Astrology was almost unknown in Greece before the time of Alexander the Great. The Greeks had no star religion and no interpretation of the stars as did the ancient civilizations in Egypt and Mesopotamia. In early Greek civilization there was only weather lore based on celestial phenomena which was used by farmers and sailors.

Theophrastus, one of Aristotle's pupils, mentioned with astonishment that it was claimed to be possible to predict not only the weather but a person's destiny based on celestial phenomena.

After Alexander's death in 323 BC, Alexandria became a cultural centre where the eastern and Greek cultures met. It was only after 300 BC that the astrological views from Mesopotamia penetrated the Greek culture to a greater extent.

Around 280 BC the Chaldean priest Berossus founded a school on the Island of Kos at which he taught (in Greek) the Chaldean lore of the stars. Kos was the perfect location for his endeavours. The island was the birthplace of Greek medicine where an Asklepion, a mystery centre dedicated to Asclepius, the god of medicine, was located. Hippocrates, the father of medicine, taught and lived there. The spirit of the Asclepian mysteries was a living presence on the island.

Berossus began to teach the old wisdom of the stars here and was soon famous throughout Greece. He made such an impression on the Athenians that they had a statue erected to him with a golden tongue as a tribute to his oratory. The school of Berossus certainly contributed a great deal to the dissemination of Chaldean star wisdom in Greece.

When eastern astrology became known in Greece, something surprising took place. Astrology seized the Greeks like a new illness seizes the inhabitants of a remote island, according to the historians. Astrology was taken up with the greatest fervour. In Greece it fell on fruitful soil as the Greeks were familiar with the planetary gods. Although they had no star religion or interpretation of the stars, no sacred books and no priests who were familiar with observing the heavens, they nevertheless marvelled at the incomparable splendour of the starry sky. In addition, the Greeks lived with divine gods whom the people got to know through poets and singers. Even before the time of Homer, the sky was personified in Uranus, the earth in Gaia, the sun in Apollo.

For Plato all the stars were divine beings who reminded human beings of their pre-birth existence. Mankind came from the world of the stars and returned there after death.

In *The Republic* Plato described in the form of a myth how the human being's destiny is defined before his birth. It is fixed in the stars at birth as an unalterable fact by the gods of fate, the Moirae, and watched over by the gods of the planets. Later the planets act as helpers for the god Moira in the fulfilment of destiny. It was Plato who first advocated the involvement of the star gods in individual human destiny. His philosophy made it clear that the fate of human beings was determined by the stars. Plato thus unintentionally laid an important foundation for the acceptance of astrological thought into Greek culture.

A second reason for the rapid acceptance of these views was the fact that there was a strong sense of the power of destiny. As the mystery of Golgotha approached, the dependency of the soul on the cosmos was felt with increasing intensity. Human destiny was considered as predetermined and inevitable.

Historians such as Bertrand Russel have shown that an all-powerful force of destiny existed in the Greek culture's attitude to life. This formed the central motif of this time, even finding expression in the Oedipus legend.

Oedipus was the son of Laius, king of Thebes, and his wife Jocasta. Even before Oedipus was born, the Oracle of Delphi had foretold that their son would kill his father and marry his mother. In order to prevent this disaster, the father Laius had his newborn son abandoned in the mountains where he was found by a shepherd who brought him up. The growing boy also learned of his terrible destiny from an oracle and tried with all his strength to prevent the fulfilment of this prophesy. But in vain

The drama of his life had to be fulfilled. He could not escape his destiny: it was inevitable.

The feeling of life being predestined led the people of the time to go to the oracle with their questions about destiny. The oracle sites were never so popular as at that time. The fact that, through their ambiguous answers, the oracles encouraged the enquirers to take on responsibility themselves had no effect.

The Greeks' familiarity with inescapable destiny led them to take up the teachings from Mesopotamia without difficulty. They succeeded in giving the birth horoscope a form which would survive for many hundreds of years.

8. Contrasting World Views

When the astrological views from Mesopotamia spread into Greece they gave rise to totally new questions. The Greek civilization belonged to the fourth post-Atlantean cultural epoch in which the intellectual or mind soul developed. The Greeks were predisposed to philosophize. They developed thinking and were compelled to seek the truth.

The omen astrology from the East flowed from a star religion, and it was quite natural for all Mesopotamians. Birth horoscopy, on the other hand, freed itself from any connection to religion. Although the Greeks could grasp the new views without difficulty they had to struggle to really understand them. The independent thinking which was beginning to emerge attempted to develop a philosophical understanding of the relationship between the human being and the world of the stars.

The question as to the nature of this relationship received various answers. A philosophical battle over astrology arose in the time after Christ, a battle which became particularly heated in relation to birth horoscopy.

The contrasting world views which existed at the time are very interesting because they persisted through the centuries. Basically three different philosophical answers were provided, originating from the Stoics, from Neoplatonism and from the church fathers. Because these answers still exist in a modified form, they ought to be mentioned here.

The world view of the Stoics

The philosophical school of the Stoics was founded by Zeno in Athens around 300 BC. His successors in the leadership of the school were Cleanthes and Chrysippus. Both came to Rome from Asia Minor and were familiar with the oriental star wisdom. Chrysippus was such a distinguished teacher in the school that it was said of him: 'The Stoics would not exist if it were not for Chrysippus.'

The school taught a strict set of laws which defined everything in the cosmos. There is *only* determinism in the universe, no freedom. Even chance does not exist. Everything occurs according to unalterable laws and even God is unable to change this.

Chrysippus made the inevitability of fate into a fundamental teaching of the Stoics. Predetermination ruled both in the destiny of the world and in that of the individual. This linked the Stoics closely to astrological paths of thought. Science observes the world of created things and calls its order — a chain of cause and effect — *necessity.* Religion looks from the standpoint of the creator and calls the order in the world *Providence.* Astrologers speak of *destiny,* fate, predestination. Necessity, Providence and destiny are therefore one and the same, only considered from different viewpoints. The Stoics viewed Providence as a spiritual principle to which human beings must submit. They had a significant effect by lending philosophical support to the interpretation of the stars.

The Stoics were not unworldly philosophers. They stood in the midst of life and were able to repeatedly adapt their ways of thinking to new social relationships and political situations. This enabled their philosophy to be accepted in the world of that day.

It is not possible to look at all the facets of this complex and versatile philosophy here, so the discussion will be confined to those elements relating to astrology.

The following phases can be identified in the development of the Stoics:

1. the early Stoics of Zeno (third and second centuries BC);
2. the middle Stoics (Poseidonius, around 100 BC);

3. the late Stoics, to which many famous Romans belonged, like Seneca and the Emperor Marcus Aurelius.

This philosophy did not result in weakness, but it actually developed strength of mind. The stoical virtues can be observed in Marcus Aurelius whose life was characterized by loyal action, courage, self-control and steadfastness.

The determinism of the Stoics contributed much to the support and spread of horoscopy. The opinion that man must fully assent to his celestial fate, accept his dependence on the stars, also met with approval in the Roman Empire. This view was later modified to the extent that the horoscope was taken as a guiding principle for life, as a life plan. The stars indicated at birth what was to be done during life.

Neoplatonism

Strongly contrasting viewpoints and philosophies to those of the Stoics first arose in the centuries after Christ. An important viewpoint was that of Neoplatonism, which wished to renew Plato's philosophy.

Neoplatonism was developed and blossomed in the second to sixth centuries after Christ. It contained a continuation of the initiation principle of the pre-Christian mysteries. Ammonius Saccas of Alexandria, whose life is not recorded directly, is considered to be the founder. We only know about him from his pupils' references.

His most famous pupil was Plotinus who formulated the philosophical system. The Neoplatonists considered themselves as faithful interpreters of Plato, not as creators of a new philosophy. However, in reality they constructed something totally new.

According to their teachings, the human being became an increasingly independent being over the course of time. This alienated him from the spiritual world. The human being therefore no longer knows whence he came: he is totally unaware of his origin.

The highest (the eternal, spiritual, good) stands *above* all contradictions. It eludes human reason and cannot be imagined. The beings who inhabit the stars are beings of pure light. They are perfect and elevated over everything which is ascribed to them in a petty belief in the stars, interpretation of the stars and star religion.

Plotinus was born around 205 in Egypt. He studied in Alexandria and moved to Persia in 242 in an attempt to get to know Indian and Persian philosophy there. He was head of a philosophy school in Rome from 244 until his death in 270.

Some of the opinions which were held by the Chaldean mystery priests reappear with Plotinus, such as a natural belief in the correspondence between the earthly world and the world of the stars. Plotinus would have found it impossible to understand earthly life without this correspondence. A meek obedience to fate or a predetermined destiny were totally alien to him, as each human being had the power to find the way back to his spiritual origin and thus shape his life in a meaningful way.

Plotinus wrote a treatise, *Are the stars causes?* in which he set down his opinions. The stars are divine beings which influence the earthly world. However, it is not the positions of the stars which determine the effects, but the beings themselves who bring about the movements in the cosmos. The human being can only get to know these beings when he rises to a knowledge of beings, to intuition. This requires higher development, purification of the soul.

This approach shows the obvious continuation of pre-Christian mystery paths. The Neoplatonic school included Iamblichus who was also dedicated to higher development. He stressed that only initiation gives the human being the chance of raising himself above the force of destiny, of liberating himself from the dictates of the stars. Iamblichus therefore made astrology part of the mysteries again.

We therefore have two opposing opinions:

1. The Stoics: the human being is determined by the cosmos. His destiny is unalterable.

2. The Neoplatonists: the human being can liberate himself from the dictates of the stars through purification of the soul and initiation.

The church fathers

A third answer was given by the church fathers, the founders of Christian church doctrine.

One of the most important Greek church fathers was Origen. Born of Christian parents in Alexandria, he was appointed leader of the famous Catechetical School at the age of eighteen. At the same time he studied Greek philosophy as a pupil of Ammonius Saccas, the founder of Neoplatonism. Throughout his life he sought a philosophical understand of Christianity. He also applied himself to the question of the link between man and the cosmos. This led him to the conviction that correspondences exist between the constellations of the zodiac and the human body. The celestial phenomena can also be omens which foretell future earthly events such as the star which announced the birth of Christ.

According to Origen, the star writing can therefore announce the will of God. However, reading this script is reserved for initiates and higher beings such as the angels.

Human destiny is not directed by the stars: they are purely an indication but have no power. Human beings can always develop their will in freedom.

Origen was the first to formulate the position of astrology within Christian belief. This led to the possibility of discussion.

Justin the Martyr — not to be confused with Justin the Gnostic — expressed himself in a similar manner. He cited Paul: 'When we were children, we were slaves to the elemental spirits of the universe' (Gal.4:3) and added: now, as Christians we are set free. For Paul, the 'elemental spirits of the universe' included the planets and signs of the zodiac and he left no doubt that through and in Christ we are freed from their domination.[1] Justin said: we are no longer children under the dictates of the stars: Christ has set us free.

The church father Tertullian objected to birth horoscopy in particular. In his opinion, the relationship between human beings and the cosmos had changed fundamentally through Christ. The dependency of human beings on the world of the stars *was* a fact *until* the appearance of Christ on earth. Through his life and death, Christ fundamentally changed the relationship of mankind to the world of the stars, for through Christ mankind's dependence on the stars had been overcome. He was indeed the saviour, the healer of the Fall. Tertullian held that belief in this was a requirement of being Christian. If, since that time, human beings continue to turn towards the stars, then they are turning towards lower beings than the Saviour himself. The Christian church calls these the fallen angels. Tertullian believed that since the appearance of Christ, there was no longer any justification for the casting of horoscopes.

The church fathers did not dispute that the stars exert influence on purely physical processes. They pointed out that the cosmos obviously affected the seasons, the rhythms of day and night. The Moon influenced the tides, the ebb and flood. Human beings, however, were no longer dependent on the stars. Man had the possibility of free will due to Christ: he could become a free being.

It will be obvious that the two other answers were unacceptable to the church fathers.

1. The answer given by the Stoics (determinism through the world of the stars) from a Christian viewpoint was only valid in pre-Christian times, as it speaks of a cosmic reality as it was before Christ's appearance on earth.
2. The answer given by the Neoplatonists attempted to continue pre-Christian mystery paths. The church fathers were bound to reject this way, as it was viewed as a path of self-redemption which denied the working of Christ and in addition was only suitable for a

> small group of elite. This way had to be condemned by the church because the redeemer had brought the possibility for *all* people to be set free from the rule of the stars.

The words of the church fathers: the redeemer came to break the power of the stars, was cited repeatedly in the Middle Ages. Christ was also frequently depicted as the vanquisher of the powers of the stars.

These three views on astrology have basically been retained throughout the centuries. Only the standpoint of the Christian church has been expressed with increasing clarity (see Chapter 11).

9. Advisers to the Caesars in Rome

Astrology was taken up in the Roman Empire in a very different way than in Greece. The Romans had no inclination for philosophy and science: they were a nation of farmers and their soldiers conquered the world. On account of the numerous wars the empire was in continual and active contact with other cultures. Not only were vast numbers of prisoners of war (for instance from Syria in 189 BC) taken to Rome as slaves, but the city attracted all who wished to seek their fortune. The simple people were fascinated by the Persian diviners, soothsayers and casters of horoscopes who came to Rome around 200 to 150 BC. The name 'Chaldean' became a generic term — with a negative connotation — for astrologers from all parts of the world.

With his strict morals, Cato cautioned against this nonsense and in 139 BC an edict was issued calling all Chaldeans to leave Rome and Italian soil within ten days, because they — according to one version — 'made a lucrative profit from the people's credulity with their bogus astrology.' However, the numerous Syrian and Greek slaves and freedmen who were tutors in Roman service were not affected by this.

Carneades of Cyrene made a strong attack on astrology. He was a Greek philosopher who came to Rome from Athens as an ambassador in 156 BC. His arguments against birth horoscopy were found to be so opposite that they were repeatedly used by opponents in the centuries following.

The most important of them were:

1. It is impossible to ascertain the exact moment of conception and birth and to make precise observations of the sky and positions of the stars for these.

2. People who were born at the same place at the same

time (particularly twins) have the same horoscope but often have very different destinies.

3. Conversely, people with the same destiny (death in battle or from mass disasters) do not have the same birth horoscope.

4. Astrologers are unable to tell from the horoscope whether it is meant for the son of a king or for a simple worker.

5. How can it be claimed that certain constellations confer particular physical features and character traits if these features apply to whole nations or races? The sign of Virgo is meant to confer fair skin, so in Ethiopia no one could be born in the sign of Virgo.[1]

Carneades' discourses on the arguments against horoscopy had a powerful effect. Young Romans thronged the halls where he spoke. But his success was limited to the educated classes, among whom horoscopy lost credibility around 130 BC. However, among the masses, faith in the omnipotence of the stars continued to grow despite the expulsion of the Chaldeans in 139 BC. A strong contrast therefore arose as regards interpretation of the stars between the opinions of the educated circles and practical application amongst the simple folk.

In 90 BC the Stoic Poseidonios of Apameia came to Rome from Greece. He was an extraordinarily well-educated man who wrote mathematical, astronomical, geographical and scientific treatises. His pupils included Julius Caesar, Cicero and Lucretius. He had an enormous influence on the intellectual life of Rome. It was due to him that horoscopy gained acceptance in educated circles.

When the Roman Republic came to an end in 30 BC and the era of the Caesars began, the Stoics' philosophy had gained the upper hand. Almost all the Caesars were convinced that human beings had a destiny determined by the stars. They believed in the importance of astrology for politics and accordingly allowed themselves to be advised by astrologers. Although several times between 30 BC and AD 100 the casting of horoscopes was forbidden by edicts and resolutions, this was done because the emperors were convinced that astrological knowledge could be used to acquire and consolidate power. They wished to use this important knowledge exclusively for themselves, and so under the Caesars astrology became a state matter.

The records provide us with many names of famous astrologers. The Egyptian astrologer Thrasyllus lived at the imperial court from AD 2 and advised Augustus and Tiberius. The latter was Emperor from AD 14 to 37 and instigated the senate's decree in AD 16. All 'Chaldeans' were expelled from Rome, any circulation of astrological books and consultation with 'Chaldeans' was forbidden. Despite this, during his reign, Tiberius continually took astrological advice from Thrasyllus. Thrasyllus' son Balbillus was court astrologer to Emperor Claudius, and accompanied him on the campaign against Britain. Balbillus was behind the decree by the senate in 52 to expel all astrologers from Italy. The fear was that they would use their knowledge to determine favourable times for rebellions and assassinations. However, all edicts and decrees were to no avail, not least because everyone knew that the emperors themselves constantly took the advice of astrologers. The fascinating history of the Roman Caesars and their court astrologers in the first century has often been described in a colourful and detailed manner.[2]

An examination of the reliable records from this period show that a relatively large number of the predictions were correct, raising the question of how this can be explained.

First, around that time people's fate was very strongly connected with the stars (see Chapter 7). The human self was not expressed as powerfully in the soul as it is nowadays. Second, the relatively large number of correct predictions must doubtless be linked to the clairvoyant faculties of the astrologers. Their success was not due to the use of better horoscope techniques or rules of interpretation but to spiritual experiences. Wilhelm Gundel, a doyen of astrological research, has pointed out that many able astrologers of the time (like Thrasyllus) came from Syria or Egypt. They were probably 'magicians' who had special faculties at their disposal. The horoscope figure was a kind of mandala for them, enabling them to reach the spiritual region where the future could be seen.

The fourth century astrologer Firmicus Maternus still had access to a ritual which enabled him to receive divine inspiration. According to Wilhelm Gundel it may be that skilful astrologers from the ancient world were characterized by:

> vividly being able to see their own or another's star destiny *in a dream*: they saw the star god who would be their or another's fate, indeed a whole birth constellation appeared before them in the dream. Thus Julian the Apostate saw the death constellation of Constantine [II] in a dream: he would die when Jupiter was in Aquarius and Saturn at 25 degrees in Virgo. In addition, there are the different forms of magical research into the future which force the gods of the stars to reveal destiny by means of various aids such as an astrological dice board, orreries, using skull divination or cup divination.[3]

There were therefore many aids for activating occult faculties at the time. The horoscope chart was also used for this.

Final acceptance of astrology

Another two edicts against astrologers were issued during the reign of Emperor Domitian. These were the last, as they were then left in peace in Rome until 297. After Domitian a new period began with the Nerva-Antonine dynasty. Interest in Greek culture grew and there was a flowering of intellectual life. A serious interest in astrology developed. While the emperors believed (as did everyone) in a celestial fate, they no longer viewed the exercise of astrology as a privilege of the emperor. They had no astrological advisers for political purposes and were well disposed towards astrology.

Hadrian was 'the astrologer on the imperial throne.' He had been initiated in Eleusis and Egypt. He was so well acquainted with the art of horoscopy that he could do without astrological advisors.

Of course there were also opponents of astrology at this time, like Favorinus, an orator and philosopher, who belonged to the circle of friends of Hadrian. Plutarch also totally rejected the casting of horoscopes in his moralistic writings.

In contrast, Vettius Valens began to put together a library of horoscopes. He had worked as an astrologer in Alexandria for a long period and taught that each person has an unalterable and predestined fate from which he cannot escape. He proudly called himself a 'soldier of destiny.' His knowledge was based on revelations which were granted him through divine Providence.[4]

However, the most significant event of that century was the publication of the *Tetrabiblos* by Ptolemy. This text, written between 138 and 147, became a manual of astrology in the western world for almost 1500 years. Ptolemy was a Greek born in Alexandria in Egypt. But his greatest influence was in Rome. His book was of great importance there for the acceptance of astrology. The Neoplatonists, especially Plotinus and his pupil Porphyrius, also contributed to this. Both lived in Rome where their philosophy was considered an important support for astrology. However, increasing numbers of charlatans appeared in the Roman Empire who spread a common form of astrology. Perhaps on account of this growing popularity of common astrology, in 297 Diocletian again issued an edict against the exercise of the 'mathematical art.' Those who cast horoscopes were called 'mathematici' at the time instead of 'Chaldeans.' The edict had as little success as the previous ones.

The rise of Christianity

In 323 Constantine the Great raised Christianity to state religion, thus preparing the way for the rise of Christianity as a world religion. This began a completely new developmental phase in cultural history, as Christianity put an end to the final offshoots of the star religion. Worship of star gods was totally alien to Christianity. Plotinus' opinion that stars are divine beings rapidly lost its importance. The threads connecting astrology to a religion of the stars were dissolved by Christian faith. Neither did the continuing effects of Ptolemy's astrology in the world of that time have anything to do with religion or gods and contributed to ending the deification of the stars. A transition took place from belief in the star gods to a scientific attitude.

This transition is shown clearly in the life and work of the above-mentioned Firmicus Maternus. Between 335–337 he wrote a textbook of astrology in Latin in eight volumes, entitled *Matheseos.* It was very popular in the Middle Ages as a guide to the theory and practice of astrology, alongside the *Tetrabiblos* of Ptolemy. In this work Firmicus Maternus speaks with conviction and reverence about the planetary gods. He still holds the old view of astrology as a religion of the stars. The god of Mercury, for example, gives astrologers the inspirational wisdom which they need. Firmicus Maternus believed that reverential recognition of these gods was essential for the practice of interpreting the stars. Because the astrologer actually associates with gods, the highest demands are placed on him. Because he consorts with the gods he must undergo a divine change, should be modest and not avaricious, not ask any forbidden questions, not associate with anyone in secret and show himself to be noble at all times.[5]

Firmicus Maternus supposedly converted to Christianity in his later years. A far-reaching change then took place in his opinions. While his *Matheseos* is filled with reverential belief in the gods, after his conversion he speaks a very different language. His treatise *De errore profanarum religionum,* written around 348, was dedicated to the sons of Constantine the Great. He urged them to ruthlessly persecute all who still believed in the old gods. Firmicus Maternus now wished to raise astrology to a science and distanced himself from belief in the possible influences of the star gods. By renouncing the old star faith, the question inevitably arose as to how interpretation of the stars can make sense without belief in the gods? What can take the place of the gods which have been overthrown?

The demand to give astrology a rational basis was made with increasing urgency in the first centuries after Christ. This task fell to the church fathers and later to scholasticism (see Chapter 11).

10. The Cult of Mithras, an Astrological Religion

In the first centuries of Christianity the cult of Mithras flourished in the Roman Empire. Originating in the east, it bore the character of a star religion. The Mithraic temples were richly decorated with cosmic symbols and a cosmic piety filled the followers. The Mithras expert F. Cumont has described the cult of Mithras as a definite 'astrological religion.' Some Mithraic priests proudly called themselves *studiosus astrologiae.* The Mithraic religion was supported by many of the Roman Caesars and had numerous followers amongst the Roman soldiers on account of its heroic character and high moral standards. The worship of Mithras, the *Sol invictus,* the unconquered sun god, spread into the furthest corners of the empire thanks to the Roman legions. During the second and third centuries after Christ the worship of Mithras developed into a world religion. For a time it was one of the strongest competitors to Christianity in the Roman Empire.

Cosmic symbols played an important role in Mithraic temples. The followers of Mithras created cult temples as a mirror of the cosmos.[1] These temples were small and the ceiling of the semicircular barrel vault often showed the blue of the sky with yellow or golden stars. Or the ceiling had small openings with lamps or torches placed behind them to create an impression of the glowing firmament.

Great importance was placed on the intimacy of the cult temples. The largest Mithraeum found to date, excavated in Romania, had a length of 26 metres and a width of 12 metres. However, most Mithraea had dimensions of less than 10 metres. There was a preference for building several small temples at one place instead of losing the intimacy. Those present during the ritual proceedings had the feeling of being in the cosmos.

The altar picture on the wall opposite the entrance gave the cult temple a distinctive character. It depicted Mithras' most important deed: the killing of the bull. Cult images show this central motif in numerous variations. The representation is often framed by a range of cosmic symbols. There are very few altar pictures which completely lack these symbols. Those which recur are the signs of the zodiac or its guardians, the planetary gods or the chariot of the Sun travelling above and the chariot of the Moon travelling below. In addition there are plant motifs, animals (lion, raven, bull, dog), etc. In the Mithras religion the connection of the human being to the cosmos was vividly experienced and cultivated.

The cult image of the killing of the bull

We can try to gain an appreciation of the cult image of the killing of the bull from the observations by Alfred Schütze in his book on Mithras.[2] He describes how the confrontation of the human being with the animal is one of the most important motifs in ancient mythology. Countless cult images, not only in Asia Minor and Ancient Egypt but also on Crete and in Greece show how human beings, heroes and gods fight against animals and dragons. Or human beings encounter sphinxes who present them with riddles or questions whose answers are a matter of life and death.

Opinions regarding the connection between man and animal are not confined to that period but also exist in our time. Since Darwin, science has pointed to the kinship of man and the animals. We are familiar with the fact that the human being has something of an animal nature in him.

The teachers of wisdom in the ancient mysteries spoke in their own way, in pictures, of the interweaving nature of man and animal. Then as now the animal was viewed as a part of the human being himself.

However, two differences in comparison with the present-day perspective must be considered.

First, the early teachers of wisdom considered not only the animal in man but,

> simultaneously counterbalanced this by pointing out the divine element which belongs to it. The god triumphing over the animal contributes a helping and redemptive third element in the human being, thus providing the balance. The human being stands between animal and divine and not only the animal nature but also the divine has to be understood as a principle residing in the human being. However, the indwelling of God in man represents a stage which was felt to be a goal for the future, only to be reached gradually.[3]

Second, for the people of ancient times,

> *everything* [was] divine — even the animal nature. The divine beings behind animals were actually worshipped as being particularly lofty and connected to the world of the stars which is why the constellations of the ecliptic were called signs of the circle of animals, the zodiac. For this reason, certain animals were considered to be sacred. But the natural forces which were felt to be great and divine in the animal kingdom, presented a danger to human beings who were meant to develop into free self-aware beings. These dull, instinctive, compulsive forces work in the realm which would nowadays be called the subconscious into which Luciferic and Ahrimanic powers had crept since the Fall. Therefore, if the animal forces in man were not to be considered 'evil' in themselves, they needed to be tamed in the ancient sense and brought under the control of other spiritual influences. The source of *these* influences was sought in the beings who were worshipped as 'sun beings' or similar gods. Their influence was only felt slowly and by degrees in as far as man gradually matured into a conscious and individual being, freeing himself more and more from the dull instinctive ties of blood and race.[4]

The human being is therefore related to the animal. He carries natural forces within himself which, however, have a lofty cosmic origin. To become human demands that this inner cosmos be spiritually tamed.

The world view of that time shows us how this inner cosmos in mankind arose. It saw man as being closely connected to the cosmos because the incarnating soul had passed through the planetary spheres before birth. From each sphere the soul had taken up particular talents. This path of the soul before birth was described around AD 400 by the Neoplatonist Macrobius in his commentary on Cicero's *Dream of Scipio* in the following words:

> The soul travels from the realm of the fixed stars down to ever lower spheres and while moving through these it is not only clothed in a body of light but also acquires all those characteristics which it will make use of on the earth: in the sphere of Saturn logical thinking and reason, in that of Jupiter vigour, in that of Mars fiery courage, in that of the Sun god the ability to perceive and to form images, desire in the sphere of Venus, the ability to speak and make itself understood in the realm of Mercury. The ability to grow and reproduce is gained in the sphere of the Moon.[5]

In his commentary from *c.* 380 on Virgil's *Aeneid,* Servius Honoratus also wrote on the view of those with knowledge of the stars 'that the souls when descending draw towards themselves: sloth from Saturn, wrath from Mars, sexual passion from Venus, greed from Mercury, the lust for power from Jupiter.'[6]

Although the descriptions of the planetary talents allow considerable scope, the idea of a pre-birth journey of this kind was widely held at the time. During life on earth, the human being therefore possessed the talents received from the cosmos before birth. When the planets were spoken of at that time this generally referred to the planetary talents and forces in human nature and less to the visible planets in the sky. The cosmic symbols in the cult images were therefore an indication of inner human nature.

The image of Mithras conquering the bull is thus an archetype of man's development. It indicates the challenge given to man of becoming lord over the cosmic forces which are active in him. The human being must triumph over these forces.

Mithras conquering the bull was not placed before men solely as an archetype of human development but was also intended as a prophecy.

> What the human being is not yet able to achieve with his own strength will be accomplished by God who thus performs a ground-breaking deed which can be emulated by the individual on a small scale if he takes Mithras as the guide for his soul. Mithras will give him the power to achieve what appears impossible.[7]

The image of Mithras conquering the bull therefore contains the ideal of becoming like Mithras. The human being can then conquer the cosmic forces in his own being and overcome the bonds to the cosmic forces.

Mithraic religion and Christianity

The clear similarity of the Mithraic religion to Christianity may be puzzling. For his followers, the Roman Mithras was the unconquered Sun god, *Sol invictus.* This found expression in hundreds of inscriptions. Christ was also the light of the world for his followers. Both Mithras and Christ were worshipped as gods of the Sun and light.

Christ had to be born in the human heart, in the words of Paul: 'it is no longer I who live, but Christ who lives in me' (Gal.2:20). The believer in Mithras also had to become like Mithras who overcomes the bull — the natural human being — in himself. Both religions stress that the human being will only find his true human dignity when he raises himself above the animal, when he grasps his spiritual self with its sunlike origin.

Alfred Schütze describes what was involved in the task of becoming like Mithras as follows:

> This made the cult of Mithras into the bearer of a progressive cultural impulse. It therefore took account of the human reality which had been developing gradually over the course of millennia: the bull nature alone was no longer enough for attaining full humanity. Something additional was needed apart from what comes easily to the human being as a divine gift without his own efforts, something arising from an even higher world but which can only be found through the greatest personal effort. Man must develop a single-minded intention from his own individual activity which will reform his 'nature' in a spiritual sense. He himself will then become Mithras who overcomes the bull. The natural human being is not yet fully human. Nature is unable to give him that which will make him fully human: it guides him to a certain stage and then leaves him there. He can only find his fulfilment as a human being himself. Without this self-realization he remains unfinished. He may bear a human face but is in truth only the incomplete model which has not attained its purpose.
>
> The figure of Mithras subduing the bull symbolizes the impulse of the human I. Mithras is not something foreign to man who approaches from outside but is to be born inside mankind. He is the representative of individual humanity, as it were, the cosmic archetype for the human self.[8]

Mithras therefore appears to be identical with Christ because Christ also represents individual humanity, as it is through him that man can find his true self. Both Christ and Mithras are seen as the guardians of the true being of man. Both give human beings the strength to free themselves from the ties to cosmic forces.

The similarities between the Mithraic religion and Christianity cannot be explained from a mutual influence. We have to assume that both religions have come about from the same or similar spiritual sources.[9]

Historically, the cult of Mithras and also Mithraic astrology can be traced back to Chaldean influences.[10] The cult of Mithras was unknown in Rome at the beginning of the era of the Caesars. Plutarch reported that the spread of the Mithraic religion began when Pompey defeated the pirates along the coast of Cilicia (Asia Minor) in 67 BC. They were sold to Italy as slaves and brought the Mithraic religion there.

In the first century Mithraism underwent a rapid spread along the Rhine as far as Britain. The earliest evidence for the cult of Mithras in the west dates from the time around AD 90, from Heddernheim (northeast of Mainz, Germany) where Roman legions were stationed. A second Mithraeum was built there only a decade later.

By the middle of the second century the cult of Mithras had spread over large areas of Europe as far as Britain. Increasing numbers of Mithraea were built between 150 and 250 and, around 250, the cult of Mithras had become a widespread religion. The last recorded founding of a Mithraic temple is from Gimmeldingen (north-west Germany) in 325.

A swing towards Christianity took place around this time. In 311 there was a tolerance edict motivated by polytheistic goals: the Christian God was recognized along with other gods. In 312, Constantine the Great viewed his victory over Maxentius as proof of the greater power of the Christian God. In the years that followed, laws in favour of Christianity increased. At the same time the other cults were gradually driven back and soon the cult of Mithras was merely tolerated.

Around 350 many Mithraic temples were closed because the exercise of the cult was forbidden on pain of death, and from 377 many temples were destroyed.

The Mithraic religion disappeared as fast as it had appeared. However, it had had an enormous effect in strengthening the consciousness that there is a relationship between human beings and the stars.

11. The Views of the Christian Church

In the first few centuries after Christ a broad range of opinions and views were held in relation to astrology and horoscopy. The most important of these were those of the Stoics, the Neoplatonists, the adherents of Mithras and the Christian church.

In the cult of Mithras the connection of man to the cosmos was experienced deeply. The numerous cosmic symbols in the cult temples are witness to the reverence and veneration which were shown to the star gods. But there is not a single indication that the adherents of Mithras were familiar with birth horoscopy or practised astrology. The cult of Mithras was a final branch of the star cults of ancient times where birth horoscopy was as yet unknown.

One of the last Roman emperors who still had a cultic relationship to the celestial gods was Septimus Severus, the first north African to become Emperor. He combined a deep reverence for the gods of the stars with the determinism of the Stoics. He did nothing without first consulting astrologers. After gaining many victories over his enemies he wished to express his gratitude to the star gods who had helped him. In their honour he had the Septizodium, a magnificent temple for the seven planetary gods, built in Rome.

Although belief in the old gods was fading fast at that time, no one doubted the power of the stars. The power of destiny was felt so intensely that astrology could enjoy huge popularity even without the great star gods. It became common practice to have your horoscope cast. There were many voices raised against belief in the determining power of the stars, promising people release from celestial fate. This prospect was held out especially by those who were connected to the old mysteries. This included the Neoplatonists who, in addition to the cult of Mithras and the Stoics, represented a strong movement in spiritual life. The world view held by the Neoplatonists had deep connections to the fundamentals of astrology. Plotinus, the main representative of this philosophy, saw the correspondence of 'above' and 'below,' of the world of the heavens and that of the earth, as the most important fundamental law in creation. It was self evident to him that the planets and stars exerted an influence on the earth. However, fatalism was rejected because every human being had the power to free himself through his own efforts and training from being bound to the stars. These kind of ideas arising from the old mysteries were always present amongst the Neoplatonists.

Stoicism, Neoplatonism and the cult of Mithras were the most important philosophical movements in the first centuries after Christ. Stoicism and Neoplatonism in particular were present in varied forms. The new Christianity had to find its place in the midst of many different views.

The truly momentous new element in Christianity was the idea of salvation. This was in sharp contrast to people's experience of astrology at the time. The views of the early church fathers have been discussed in Chapter 8. In what follows the most relevant and most fully developed views of the Christian church up to the dawn of the consciousness soul era around 1400 will be presented: those of Augustine and Thomas Aquinas.

Augustine

Augustine was bishop of North Africa. He is the most famous of what are known to this day as the church fathers. His numerous writings exerted a huge influence on the Christian church in the west and his opinion was authoritative on many issues for centuries.

In his *Confessions* he wrote that in his youth he studied astrology diligently. In his later work, *Of the City of God,* he argued that, in his opinion, it is possible to predict the future with the aid of the stars. It is perfectly possible to make statements about a person's destiny from horoscopes.

When asked how this *praescientia futurorum,* this 'prior knowledge of the future' is possible, Augustine answered: 'It is possible, because God knows the future. God knows everything, he is omniscient. But man should not presume to penetrate to this divine knowledge. And this is just exactly what the astrologers claim to do.'

So human beings can predict the future with the help of the stars. Although this is possible, Augustine holds it to be unacceptable. Why should this be? Augustine asked: *who* gives mankind this knowledge of the future? It can only be demons who give this knowledge to human beings. God does not impart this knowledge of the future to mankind because he wishes to let human beings become free. The human being should become someone who makes his own decisions, out of his own strength, and not someone who is told what he should do. However, demons can take possession of this knowledge of the future and give it to mankind.

According to the views of the time, demons were angels who had fallen with Lucifer, whom God had permitted in creation and who used their power to lead mankind astray. Anyone who tried to acquire knowledge of the future with the aid of stars was turning to these demons, to beings of a lower order, to the 'enemies of God' as Augustine called them.

Augustine's opinion was authoritative for many centuries. Eight hundred years later, in 1265, Thomas Aquinas was able to follow on from this.

Thomas Aquinas

Thomas Aquinas was the most outstanding thinker of the Middle Ages. His thoughts had a tremendous impact on account of his teaching activity and his numerous books. They influenced thinking not only within the Catholic Church but their effects were felt throughout Central European culture.

None of Thomas Aquinas' works gives a systematic treatment of his opinion on astrology. His views come from many remarks which emerge scattered throughout his works. In her dissertation Eva Fleischmann-Kessler has tracked down these statements in Thomas' writings and provided a commentary on them.[1] What follows is based on Eva Fleischmann-Kessler's fundamental observations.

She describes how Thomas Aquinas' views on astrology are connected not only to his opinion of the cosmos but also to his opinion of mankind. Thomas believed that the human being has the option of free choice in his behaviour. He possesses this possibility for free choice 'thanks to his ability of critical reasoning which sees several possibilities, can view something from different sides and therefore does not determine the will one-sidedly.' Freedom of choice is nevertheless:

> only guaranteed when the human being makes use of this possibility for using reason and so raises himself above his physical restrictions into the purely spiritual realm ... However, if the human being follows his instinctual or situation-dependent inclinations, as is always the case for animals, then he allows himself to be determined by physical factors and cannot act in freedom.

Thomas Aquinas therefore distinguished clearly 'between human behaviour tied to the physical and that which is not bound physically, which is purely spiritual.'

This distinction is very important in relation to the influence of the stars, because,

> as bodies, the stars can only work directly on physical matter, that is on processes in the physical material world. Manifestations of a spiritual or psychological nature are only subject to their influence in as far as they are bound to the physical ... The heavenly bodies can therefore only work on the human being to the extent that he is bound to physical factors, to the degree that his functions belong to the plant and animal realm ... Thomas stressed that it lies within the power of the human will to follow

> emotional inclinations or to reject them, in accordance with his rational insight. The freedom to choose and decide is therefore guaranteed in principle, but Thomas takes the pessimistic view that the majority of people follow emotional drives and that only the wise, thanks to their reason, can withstand their passions ... Thomas concedes that astrologers often predict human actions correctly, especially collective events such as the outcome of wars. However, he emphatically forbade astrological predictions which relate to future human action. He justified this ban on the basis that such predictions would make the human being equal to the other creatures whose behaviour is almost completely determinate and by so doing would deny what is specifically human, that is, the possibility of freedom and self determination.

These are Fleischmann-Kessler's basic observations on Thomas Aquinas' attitude to astrology.

Thomas naturally agreed with the influence of the stars on the animal kingdom, on the plant kingdom, on the weather, the harvest and everything which is dependent on physical and natural causes. In his day astrological rules, particularly those relating to the weather, were familiar to all levels of society. Thomas mentioned how astrologers made correct weather forecasts in relation to the occurrence of droughts and rainfall using observations of the stars. A great deal is subject to the influence of the stars in the kingdoms of nature. Only in the human realm is there freedom and self determination.

Thomas' opinion on astrology is also expressed in a letter which he wrote to his friend Reginald of Piperno in answer to a question on this subject. Thomas wrote:

> Because you have asked me to write to you about whether it is permissible to make use of the decisions of the stars I would like to comply with your request and have tried to write down what is taught by the holy teachers ... In the fifth chapter of the *City of God* Augustine [said]: 'It is not in the least absurd to claim that some heavenly influences

> of the stars penetrate to the various bodies.' If therefore someone makes use of astrology to predict natural physical effects such as a storm or good weather, the health or illness of the body, the fruitfulness or poverty of the harvests or similar things which are dependent on physical and natural causes, this seems in no way to be a sin. Because all men make use of observations of the heavenly stars in relation to such effects. Just as the country folk sow and reap at a particular time which they observe from the course of the Sun; sailors avoid setting sail at full Moon and even during the waning Moon; physicians carefully observe the critical days for illnesses which are also determined according to the course of Sun and Moon, it is also no offence to make use of astrology for some more occult observations of the stars in relation to physical effects.
>
> But the one thing which must be grasped clearly is that the human will is never subject to the necessity of the stars, for then free will would be destroyed. And then the human being could be charged neither with his good deeds as profit nor with his bad deeds as debt. Therefore every Christian must first and foremost grasp what is dependent on the human will, in other words all the deeds of man, is not subject to the necessity of the stars.

Thomas then cites Augustine who, amongst others, said that whoever questions the stars because he wishes to turn to the them, enters a pact with demons, or (as expressed by Thomas) with 'tempting spirits who may well be allowed to know much that is true about matters of time.' A Christian should avoid a pact with demons and:

> follow the words of the Apostle [Paul] in the First Letter to the Corinthians [Chapter 10]: 'I do not want you to be partners with demons.' And therefore it is correct to regard it as a great sin to follow the judgment of the stars in that which is dependent on the will of man.[2]

In his *Summa Theologica* Thomas states his opinion that: 'the fact that astrologers can predict the truth in most cases, only proves that few people make use of the possibility of their freedom.'[3]

The demons

It can strike us as strange that in those days it was so natural to speak of demons, of inspiration and intuition which came from good or evil beings. However, we must bear in mind that the people of that time still had a feeling for such things. They could still experience the source of intuition and ideas.

If you ask someone nowadays, 'Where do your thoughts come from?' the usual scientific answer is, 'From the brain.' This answer only became possible when a scientific consciousness arose. Previously, before the advent of science, people still felt that inspiration descended into their thinking from the spiritual world.

Nowadays we would put it in modern language as follows: naturally the interpretation of horoscopes is *not* a rational matter, not something that comes about through purely logical inference. A particular aspect of the stars permits many interpretations. Ideas, inspiration are needed in order to select the correct one. Anyone who wishes to interpret a horoscope looks unconsciously for intuition, otherwise he would never arrive at a result. He turns to beings who can inspire him. In the language of Thomas Aquinas: 'He requests intuition from the world of spiritual beings and needs to protect himself from becoming an associate of demons.'

At that time it was still absolutely clear that astrology is an 'esoteric science' because it obtains its knowledge from the spiritual world. The way in which Thomas Aquinas viewed the matter shows that the possibility of freedom, the option of a choice of actions, was experienced with increasing force as the era of the intellectual or mind soul progressed. After 1400 the gradual development of the consciousness soul began. It was accompanied by a process of human individualization. The self-awareness and maturity of individual human beings increased greatly. The awareness of freedom linked to this will continue to increase in the course of the era of the consciousness soul.

12. The Flowering and Decline of Astrology

At the beginning of the fifteenth century a new era began in Europe with the development of the consciousness soul. Voyages of discovery (Columbus, Vasco da Gama and others) opened up completely new parts of the world. Copernicus put forward a new picture of the cosmos. The Reformation began a liberation from old authorities.

The search for the new turned to the past for inspiration. The Renaissance, a rebirth of ancient culture, reached its highpoint between 1450 and 1520. Leonardo da Vinci, Michelangelo and Raphael renewed the Greek ideals of beauty. The interest in astrology from earlier centuries also experienced a revival. This interest was further encouraged by the invention of the art of printing (in 1459). Texts which had previously been accessible to only a small elite could now be printed and found wide circulation.

Within a short space of time astrology and horoscopy became familiar through all levels of society. However, with popularization it became more superficial, because the material which was printed had to appeal to the general public and be easy to understand. Almanacs with astronomical, astrological and liturgical information were in great demand. They contained descriptions of astrological symbols (signs of the zodiac, planetary gods) and sometimes also predictions about the weather, politics, the harvest and potential epidemics.

From 1500 onwards astrological textbooks from earlier centuries, sometimes with commentaries, were printed (for instance, Ptolemy, Manilius, Firmicus Maternus). The casting of horoscopes became much easier with printed tables showing daily positions of the planets. In 1550, some almanacs had print runs of 100,000.

Astrology was not considered an 'esoteric' matter in the sixteenth century as it fitted with the pre-Copernican view of the world. The Earth was seen as the centre of a total of ten cosmic spheres. In this approach the outermost sphere or the furthest heaven forms the empyreum, the home of the blessed and the angels. The empyreum surrounds the crystal sphere where the daily movement of the stars from east to west takes place. These spheres are kept in motion by the highest divine beings. The next sphere is the heaven of the fixed stars followed towards the centre by the seven planetary spheres (from Saturn to the Moon) with their irregular motions that were caused by spiritual beings.

Astronomy and astrology were a unified field of knowledge as long as this view of the world was generally accepted. Cosmic influences on the events on earth were nothing extraordinary, because spiritual beings affected the earth from the cosmic spheres. This unified field of knowledge of astronomy and astrology was taught in universities up to 1650 and was part of general education. The sciences were known as arts at that time and astrological concepts (signs of the zodiac, planets) were naturally amongst the arts taught at universities. Every student had to acquire a knowledge of astrological symbolism.

The doctrine of signatures was popular: the form and function of objects are expressions of cosmic formative principles, which reappear in analogous things of related nature. Thus minerals, plants, trees, herbs, animals, metals, colours, human characteristics etc. can be assigned to one of the seven planets (the five visible ones together with Sun and Moon). Professions were also assigned to the planets; for instance, the army to Mars, artists to Venus, scholars to Saturn, the clergy to Jupiter, merchants to Mercury, sailors to the Moon. The planets were seen as patron saints of these professional groups. An astrological inventory could be made of the entire world using cosmic symbolism. Due to the doctrine of signatures, astrology became widely disseminated in public life, politics, art and literature, and horoscopy was able to spread in its wake.

The flowering of horoscopy during the fifteenth and sixteenth centuries was aided by the support given to astrology by the popes and princes. Pope Paul II even announced in his coronation speech (1464) that he believed in the correctness of astrological predictions. Pope Sixtus IV and Alexander VI also took advice from permanently employed astrologers. Pope Paul III never undertook a journey without first having asked astrologers about favourable dates.

Around 1650 a change took place. All sympathy for astrology as a serious matter disappeared within a short time. It was viewed as superstition and lies. In 1670 teaching of astrology had almost disappeared from German universities. In France in 1666, the members of the French Academy of Sciences were forbidden to study astrology by Jean-Baptiste Colbert, the minister of finance. Louis XIV followed this with a ban in France on all astrological calendars and almanacs (1682). In 1688 the church also banned all astrological literature. Even the philosopher Leibniz who was so tolerant in later years declared that 'he only scorns that which comes down to pure deception, such as the art of astrological prediction.'[1] The study of horoscopes soon became a contemptible matter. What led to this reversion?

The Copernican view of the world

The Copernican picture of the world decisively changed the view of the cosmos. Did the advent of this world view undermine belief in astrology? What was the significance of this new picture of the cosmos for the interpretation of the stars?

Copernicus was a minor cleric in the cathedral chapter in Frombork on the Vistula Lagoon (now in north-east Poland) who studied astronomical matters. He considered Ptolemy's geocentric world view to be too complicated. The planetary spheres around the Earth were still a living reality for Ptolemy but the mathematical treatment of the actual planetary movements was very complex. The retrograde motion of the planets could be explained mathematically with relative ease, but the differences in size and brightness of the planets caused by the changing distances from the Earth made the mathematical interpretation extraordinarily complex. Copernicus could not believe that God would have created such a complicated world system. He had doubts about the generally accepted teaching on the central position of the Earth in the planetary system. In his major work, *De Revolutionibus Orbium Coelestium,* he placed the sun in the centre and let the planets orbit the sun. He saw this heliocentric world view as an idea which the Creator had placed in the world. As a pious man he wished to contribute to the understanding of this divine creative idea. He certainly had no wish to provoke a philosophical revolution, and had no inkling of the later effects of his world view and of a ban by the church. He dedicated his book to Pope Paul III in complete naivety, although friends advised him against publishing his work.

It was only at his death in 1543 that his work was published. The book did not evoke an immediate reaction from the church. Certainly, many people foresaw that the new world view would change the cosmos into an infinitely large physical space in which there was no longer any room for God. However, it took almost a century before the church condemned the teachings of Copernicus, and Galileo had to renounce them in 1633.

What were the consequences of the Copernican world view for astrology? Ptolemy had not only viewed the Earth as the stationary centre in space but had also imagined the cosmos qualitatively. The world of the stars could still be inhabited by living spiritual beings. The Copernican world view replaced a cosmos inhabited by spiritual beings with a purely mathematical frame of reference. A complete de-deification of the heavens was set in motion.

Did this pose a threat to astrology? Contrary to expectations this was not the case. Although the gods disappeared from the cosmos, the new system was welcomed by many astrologers. They viewed the strict order of the heliocentric world view as powerful support for the existence of astrological relationships and began to refer to the new world view in their theories.

It was in fact astrologers, for example his pupil Rheticus, who urged Copernicus to publish. Without doubt the Copernican world view encouraged rather than damaged belief in astrology in the sixteenth and seventeenth centuries.

Reasons for the setback

What was it that caused a setback in the esteem accorded to astrology in the seventeenth century? Several reasons can be given for this.

The art of printing was a tremendous invention which had significant consequences. On the one hand, textbooks were printed which encouraged familiarity with astrology amongst scholars and in universities. On the other hand descriptions of astrology which could be generally understood now appeared and everyone could cast horoscopes and publish predictions.

The art of printing also led to the emergence of abuse and dilettantism in the realm of astrology that grew during the Thirty Years' War (1618–48). This war caused devastation on a vast scale in Central Europe resulting in cultural degeneration. In the wake of general uncertainty and vulgarizing of traditions, charlatans had free reign. Everything that happened (bad harvests, illnesses, epidemics of the plague, etc.) was blamed on the stars without further explanation. The name 'influenza' was coined because it was assumed that this was caused by the influence of the stars.[2] Astrology was brought into disrepute through abuse of star interpretation, predictions which were not fulfilled, etc. Without doubt the invention of printing and the thirty years' war brought discredit upon astrology. But the crucial reason for the decline in astrology has to be sought elsewhere. This reason was the emergence of a completely new opponent: natural science.

The emergence of natural science

In the sixteenth and seventeenth centuries people's interest moved from the metaphysical to the physical. The study of nature, the expansion of knowledge based on facts began its triumphant progress. Galileo, physicist, mathematician and thinker, marked the beginning of this development. His discovery of the laws of gravity led to the founding of mechanics. He used a telescope to observe the nature of the surface of the Moon, the sunspots and the 'three-bodied' Saturn which was later identified as a ring. After the discovery in 1610 of the four moons of Jupiter he publicly professed his belief in the Copernican theory. This led to opposition from the church. The question arose as to whether the theory of the motion of the Earth around the Sun can be reconciled with the scriptures.

Galileo tried to find the empirically definable causes of the phenomena. At the same time he was a deeply religious man. His devout nature told him that God had given mankind the Bible for their faith, the book of revelation. For science, God gave mankind the book of nature. The task of theology is therefore to look for and fathom the revelations of the godhead in the holy writings. The task of natural scientists is to seek the divine in nature and read the book of nature. There empiricism is the source of all knowledge. Because Galileo perceived the book of nature to be written in mathematical language, he believed that only a mathematical approach could lead to knowledge.

The emerging natural science was therefore founded on an exact basis.

> *Only what can be measured is scientifically valuable,* because it is only through measuring that it is possible to *compare* the perceptions with one another and so *arrange them in a system.* Therefore only measurable quantities can be the objects of true research which would otherwise remain nothing more than a collection of material without any meaning. Measuring is the basis of all methodical research in nature, because only this can lead to useful knowledge.[3]

Since Galileo natural scientists have applied the maxim 'What can be measured must be measured and what cannot be measured must be made measurable.'

The establishment of this principle had far-reaching consequences. In the course of the following centuries the scope for measurement was continuously expanded. The scientific, the measurable, claimed to be the only correct and true reality. This brought all non-measurable phenomena into disrepute. The sharp division between measurable phenomena, which are of interest to science and non-measurable phenomena, which science considers irrelevant, had far-reaching consequences for the reputation of astrology. Astronomy and astrology, which up to that point had been viewed and taught as a unity, now became two separate areas of knowledge. Astronomy was developed further as an exact science. There was only contempt for the non-measurable relationships in astrology.

Astrology did not fit into the scientific mode of observing the world. It remained outside the realm of natural science and was therefore soon excluded from the reigning world view. In the pre-Copernican world view the Earth was the centre surrounded by cosmic spheres where spiritual beings had their home. Spiritual beings worked on the earth from these spheres, giving astrology its basis. With the decline of this world view, astrology rapidly became an alien element in prevailing culture. The fact that the astronomers Tycho de Brahe and Kepler continued to cast horoscopes was seen as their private business.

13. Boundaries of Knowledge

In his book on Galileo, Johannes Hemleben describes how there was really only *one* science in the Middle Ages, theology (also called the 'queen of all sciences'). This queen had assigned her maidservants — philosophy, medicine and jurisprudence — the relevant tasks. Natural science was not a separate discipline at the time, only becoming an independent subject in the seventeenth century when it developed its own research methods. These were characterized by precision and objectivity, an approach which was soon applied to all visible phenomena. However, the required restriction to measurable phenomena entailed a significant limitation on the field of research. A gulf began to emerge 'between the original mother and her child, between theology as a science of faith based on revelation and the science of nature.'[1]

The outcome of scientific development was a growing awareness of the gulf between the world of knowledge and the world of faith, between knowledge of the physical world and knowledge of the spiritual world.

This development was continued by Isaac Newton, the English physicist and mathematician who, amongst other things, discovered the law of gravity. Newton, however, was not only a scientist but wrote extensively on theological matters. For Newton an omnipresent God was revealed in nature and in the books of the Bible. He saw two paths to knowledge: one as a natural scientist and one as a biblical scholar.

These two paths obviously had different research methods. Physicists support their findings with verifiable facts. But there are questions which go beyond physics, such as, 'Why is it that everything in nature is arranged in a meaningful way? Where do the order and beauty which we can see in nature come from?'

Questions like these belong to the realm of metaphysics. Newton kept physics and metaphysics strictly separate because of the difference in their methods. The resulting separation of physics and metaphysics has been taken for granted since then. A century later this led to a conversation between Napoleon and the astronomer Pierre-Simon Laplace in which Napoleon asked Laplace why he had not once mentioned the Creator in his major work *(Mécanique Céleste).* Laplace answered: *'Sire, je n'avais pas besoin de cette hypothèse-là'* (Sir, I have no need for that hypothesis).

Nothing contributed so decisively to the separation between knowledge and belief in the eighteenth century as Newton's scientific work. The question of how the world of earthly facts was related to the spiritual world had occupied Thomas Aquinas four hundred years prior to this. But now the earthly and heavenly worlds were experienced as two different realms which each required their own approach in order to be understood. Natural science had only developed a research method for the earthly phenomena: these methods were not suitable for spiritual realities. The realities of the spiritual world had to be believed because there are limits to human knowing. In the nineteenth century Emil du Bois-Reymond was to view these limits to knowledge as insurmountable.[2]

This gradually increasing awareness of the boundaries of knowledge was the outcome of a long evolutionary process during the dark age. During this period man had to lose his awareness of the spiritual world in order to acquire freedom (see Chapter 1). He gained knowledge of the natural world and through this became a self-aware citizen of the earth who was able to use technology to manipulate the physical world. The price which he had to pay for this was the loss of awareness of the spiritual world, including the spiritual world of the stars. While Dante was still able to describe the human being's passage through the planetary spheres in his life after death, this was now replaced by the astrophysical view of the cosmos.

The Rosicrucians

The loss of awareness of the spiritual world was especially painful for those who sought and cultivated a relationship to it. This was particularly so for the Rosicrucians whose society was founded by Christian Rosenkreutz. He lived from 1378 to 1484, thus reaching the age of 106. His life was described in the later Rosicrucian writings. The *Fama Fraternitatis* (1614) reports on the discovery of his grave a hundred and twenty years after his death. His body was still completely intact. *The Chymical Wedding of Christian Rosenkreutz* describes the process of his initiation which took place in 1459 when he was 81.

The aims of the Rosicrucians at that time were a source of continual misunderstanding. They were often incorrectly labelled as mystics, that is as people who sought the spiritual along an *inner* path. However, the Rosicrucians' writings indicate the opposite. They knew that the development of the consciousness soul had to take place through coming to terms with the realities of the world of the senses, with outer nature. They wished to prevent development towards a materialism devoid of spirit, because otherwise human beings would no longer be able to find the way to the spirit at the end of the dark age. They did not seek the spirit on the inward path like the mystics, but on the outer path, in nature. Their aim was not a 'mystical wedding,' the connection to spiritual powers within the human being, but a 'chymical wedding,' that is, the soul's connection to the spiritual powers active in nature.

Those who sought the spirit in nature were known as alchemists at the time. They were, however, involved in something totally different from present-day chemistry. The alchemists knew that the spirit can only be found in nature when the soul is purified and metamorphosed. Their search was simultaneously an inner schooling.

Alchemy has ancient roots. Older writings attribute alchemy to Hermes Trismegistus who was also the founder of the star mysteries in ancient Egypt. It is supposed that the Rosicrucians were also familiar with the cosmic teachings of Hermes Trismegistus. The *Chymical Wedding* describes how a view of a 'spiritual astronomy' presented itself to Christian Rosenkreutz during his initiation.

The Rosicrucians felt sorrow at the approaching centuries in which it would be impossible to maintain a connection to the true spiritual world. A spiritually real relationship to the star world would also come to an end. They viewed it as their task to awaken and develop forces in the soul which would enable a new relationship to the spiritual world at the end of the dark age.

The views of the Italian philosopher and scholar Pico della Mirandola can provide insight into how the Rosicrucians of that time experienced the limits of knowledge and their attitude to the world of the stars. Outwardly Mirandola knew nothing of Christian Rosenkreutz or his brothership, nevertheless his ideas are very informative with regard to the spiritual atmosphere of his time and the aims of the Rosicrucians.

Giovanni Pico della Mirandola

Pico della Mirandola wrote a comprehensive polemical treatise against divinatory, that is predictive astrology, which was only published after his death. Pico was very well versed in and a supporter of astrology. He researched the astrological propositions of his day very thoroughly, particularly those relating to medicine. For example, if numerous gall bladder disorders appeared in a particular year this was caused by the evil effect of Mars. Pico observed that an astrologer considers a disorder like this in quite a different way from a doctor. The astrologer looks upwards to the world of the stars while the doctor examines the patient's body. He considers the patient's constitution, lifestyle, state of mind, etc. The doctor does *not* look to the remoter cosmic influences in the world of the stars but makes his judgment according to the obvious causes in the human being. He looks for the causes in the patient.

Pico's question was: 'Are the astrologers wrong?' His answer was that both are true. There are direct obvious perceptible causes. There are *also* remote cosmic causes in the background. However, according to Pico, for his diagnosis the doctor should use the most obvious causes which he can find in the patient.

Rudolf Steiner summarized Pico's convictions about the world of the stars in one of his lectures as follows:

> He established how everything that happens on earth — stones and rock coming into being, plants living and growing and bearing fruit, animals living their life — how all this cannot be attributed to the forces of the earth. If anyone were to think ... the forces of the earth produce what is on the earth, he would have quite a wrong notion of the matter. The true view, according to Pico della Mirandola, is that up there are the stars and what happens in the earth all depends on the stars. One must look up to the heavens, if one wants to understand what happens on earth. Speaking in the sense of Pico della Mirandola we should have to say: you give me your hand, my brother man, but it is not your feeling alone that causes you to give me your hand, it is the star standing above you that gives you the impulse to hold out your hand to me. Ultimately everything that is brought about has its source in the heavens, in the cosmos; what happens on earth is but the reflection of what happens in the heavens.[3]

What is unusual about Pico is that he states this as a firm belief and *at the same time* says: 'although there are cosmic causes, man should nevertheless use the most obvious causes. Human beings are obliged *not* to look to the celestial causes but only to the closest causes on the earth.' This is completely characteristic of his view. Rudolf Steiner's comment on this was:

> Note well what it is we have before us here. For the first time we are confronted with the idea of 'boundaries' to knowledge in a very curious form but, I would say, in a form which is still human in character. Later, in Kant, in

> du Bois-Reymond, you will find it said that the human being cannot cross the boundaries of knowledge, this being based on an inner necessity. This is not the case with Pico della Mirandola in the fifteenth century. He says: 'What is on earth has undoubtedly come about through cosmic causes, but man is called upon to forego knowledge of these cosmic causes. He has to limit himself to the earth.' ... This is a spiritual event in the history of culture of the greatest imaginable importance.

What Pico della Mirandola presents is the inner attitude of the emerging consciousness soul. This develops in the physical world, through the phenomena of nature and is therefore devoted to the world of the senses. The earthly world is a school in which the consciousness soul develops its faculties. The faculties for higher perception required to gain knowledge of the spiritual world can also be developed only in and through the world of the senses.[4] The emerging consciousness soul must at first — until the end of the dark age — confine itself to the earthly realm.

The Rosicrucians in particular consciously relinquished higher knowledge. In the second half of the fifteenth century a small group of Rosicrucians even deliberately and voluntarily sacrificed the star wisdom in a formal ritual act. Those who made this sacrifice knew of the spiritual beings of the hierarchies present above human beings. They distinguished three groups of spiritual beings: the first hierarchy (Seraphim, Cherubim and Thrones), the second hierarchy (Kyriotetes, Dynameis, Exousiai) and the third hierarchy (Archai, Archangels and Angels). They viewed the aim of creation as the formation of a fourth hierarchy, that of mankind.[5] The new being to be created, man, was intended to become the bearer of freedom. However, spiritual beings could only give mankind the possibility of freedom. This possibility had to be taken up by human beings themselves.

The Rosicrucians were convinced that the development of this freedom was endangered by the fact that, through the Fall, mankind had descended too far into the material world. This danger could only be averted by humanity freely relinquishing higher knowledge until the end of the dark age. The sacrifice of star wisdom mentioned above was made by individuals who still had a connection to the spiritual world. They performed a formal ritual act which Rudolf Steiner described as follows:

> Men stood before a kind of altar and said: 'We now resolve to feel responsible not only for ourselves and our community, or our nation, or the people of our time; we resolve to feel responsible for all men who have ever lived on earth, to feel that we belong to the whole of mankind. And we feel that mankind has deserted the rank of the fourth hierarchy and has descended too deeply into matter [for the Fall was understood in this sense] and in order that man may be able to return to the rank of the fourth hierarchy, may be able to find in freedom of will what Gods have tried to find for him and with him in earlier times, let the higher knowledge be offered up for a period of time ... [The spiritual world accepted the sacrifice and] the impulse to freedom was thereby made possible for man from out of the spiritual world.[6]

This sacrifice paved the way for a resurrection of the star wisdom at the end of the dark age.

The attitude of mind of the Rosicrucians which led to this sacrifice can be seen not only in Pico della Mirandola but also in contemporaries such as Agrippa von Nettesheim.

Agrippa von Nettesheim

Agrippa von Nettesheim was born in Cologne in 1486 and studied medicine and law. In 1507 his spiritual search took him to Paris where he regularly attended a secret society. Three years later he also came into contact with the famous learned abbot Johannes Trithemius von Sponheim in Würzburg. The same year he wrote his first work, *De Occulta Philosophia,* which is evidence of an astonishing versatility and knowledge of literature. It circulated in many transcripts and formed the basis for his fame.

Because he himself felt the work to be immature, it was only in 1530 that he decided to have it printed.[7]

Agrippa's life was an expression of his versatility: he was active as a physician, lawyer, philosopher, diplomat and writer. In the years between 1526 and 1529 he wrote his famous treatise on the boundaries of human cognitive ability, *De Incertudine et Vanitate Scientiarum* (Of the Uncertainty and Vanity of the Sciences).

In this work he expressed disappointment about the science of his day which repeatedly tried to imagine spiritual processes or effects for outer natural events. The spiritual was projected into the physical phenomena. Outer facts were interpreted as portents of the future. Agrippa fought for a true natural science. He wished to explain the phenomena of nature not from spiritual causes or as the effects of spiritual beings but sought natural causes as the basis for a science of nature. He also considered it necessary to have knowledge of spiritual realities beyond natural science. However, this would only be possible based on a true natural science. Like his contemporary Paracelsus, he saw knowledge of nature as the true basis for knowledge of the spirit.

Agrippa had, as he said, 'imbibed [astrology] with his mother's milk' and studied it in depth. This lead him to the discovery that interpreting horoscopes is not a matter of logical reason but a creative process requiring inspiration. Statements about constellations are always connected to ideas, to inspiration. These come from the spiritual world but are gathered by the astrologer. Agrippa came to realize that, as a result of the Fall, the human spirit had become incapable of receiving clear inspiration from the spiritual world in the right way. Statements about stars were inevitably mixed with misunderstandings and illusions. Agrippa believed that, through the effects of the Fall, the human being had become receptive to inspirations and ideas from lower beings spreading deception. Although true predictions were still possible, the practice of horoscope interpretation showed that demons had succeeded in spreading delusions. In later years Agrippa increasingly distanced himself from horoscopy.

A characteristic of the emerging consciousness soul was that it became increasingly difficult to judge whether ideas came from good spirits or from demons. Were the ideas correct or misleading? This uncertainty provoked anxiety in the soul. This fearful mood appeared particularly in those who strove for knowledge. They said to themselves, 'We can no longer judge whether spiritual inspiration is of a good or bad kind. Certainty of knowledge of the spiritual world can no longer be achieved, so we shall restrict ourselves to knowledge of the world of the senses.' This was not felt as a personal powerlessness but as a condition affecting mankind.

Feelings of this kind were prominent in the fifteenth and sixteenth centuries. They awakened an awareness of the fact that mankind had reached a stage in its development in which it was necessary to sacrifice knowledge of the spiritual world. These feelings and attitudes formed the spiritual atmosphere in which the star wisdom was sacrificed by the Rosicrucians.

14. Astrology in the Age of Natural Science

Natural science started to develop with increasing conviction from the sixteenth century onwards. Its findings spread rapidly and influenced opinions about the world and the cosmos. Astrology had to come to terms with natural science to an ever increasing degree. However, accusations that astrology was a scam, superstition and unscientific were unable to undermine its existence. There were astrologers such as Nostradamus who did not work according to scientific methods at all but who were nonetheless very successful because they possessed visionary gifts.

Those who sought a scientific basis for astrology took a very different approach, attempting to reconcile astrology and natural science. Philipp Melanchthon belonged to this school.

Those who viewed astrology as belonging to occultism took a third approach, believing that astrology should be based on a science of the spirit. This last approach can be viewed as the precursor to what would only become possible after the end of the dark age. Paracelsus, for example, belonged to this group.

These three approaches are very different and will be described in more detail below.

Visionary astrologers

In the sixteenth century there were astrologers who became famous due to the accuracy of their predictions.

The French physician, astrologer and seer Michel de Nostredame, also known as Nostradamus, became famous. He caused a great sensation by his prophecy for the year 1559 made far in advance. This was that Henry II of France was to be killed in a duel. People ridiculed this prediction, but it turned out to be true. At a tournament in 1559 the king was fatally wounded by a spear in a duel.

Nostradamus had the reputation of being an astrologer. However, his visionary ability must definitely be taken into account in relation to his predictions. From his house he had a clear view of the night sky and could immerse himself for hours in the sight of the starry heavens. Pictures of future events came to him which he wrote down in quatrains (poems of four lines). His dark, equivocal *Centuries* as they were called, each comprising one hundred of these quatrains, were passed from one person to the next.

He also possessed remarkable intuition when establishing the cause of illnesses and treating his patients. Important contemporaries such as Catherine de' Medici and Charles IX of France consulted him on medical matters.

The Italian astrologer Lucas Gauricus also became famous on account of his accurate predictions. He was called 'the prince of astrologers' because of his reputation for never being wrong. He was the astrological advisor to several popes. In 1493 he prophesied that the then fourteen-year-old Giovanni de Medici would become pope, which he then later did as Leo X. As an astrologer Gauricus was also known to have access to a high degree of visionary ability. He was appointed bishop by Pope Paul III on account of his many services.

Tycho de Brahe was not only a great astronomer but also astonished his contemporaries with horoscope interpretations which came true. His visionary powers were evident even at the age of twenty when he accurately predicted the death of the sultan Suleiman to within a few days. According to Rudolf Steiner, he acquired this ability from an instinctive element of his being connected to an earlier life on earth.[1]

So at this time there were very successful astrologers who undoubtedly possessed a visionary capacity that contributed more to their success than did their knowledge of astrological systematics. These astrologers with clairvoyant talents spent little time on calculations and exactness for their horoscope interpretation. This even applied to Tycho de Brahe. The sky for him was a great book containing eternal truths and he attached great importance to his intuition when reading this heavenly script.

Scientifically based astrology

A very different attitude is apparent amongst those who saw astrology as part of natural science. Their wish was to give astrology a scientific basis.

One such was Philipp Melanchthon, a friend of Luther. He was a keen astrologer and translated Ptolemy's *Tetrabiblos* into Latin (1553). Melanchthon considered astrology to be an essential part of classical education. In a speech on the dignity of astrology *(oratio dignitate astrologiae)* at the University of Wittenberg in 1535, he put the case for his desire to give astrology a scientific foundation.[2] He wanted to establish it as a branch of physics. He later had his lecture at Wittenberg University printed under the telling title *Initia doctrinae physicae.* This 'physical doctrine' was totally compatible with Christian faith for him. He could not entertain any division of faith and knowledge. He believed that God exercised his omnipotence in two ways: by direct means and by means of natural forces, including the heavenly bodies. The constellations influence the human being and his destiny, but the spiritual in man is not affected by this. He can master the sidereal influences by means of his reason. Melanchthon's opinions are very similar to those of Thomas Aquinas, except that the former's astrology is founded in the scientific realm.

Francis Bacon, the founder of experimental science, wished not only to describe nature but also to rule it. He coined the phrase, 'Knowledge is power.' He viewed astrology as something 'so full of superstition that it is scarcely possible to find anything sensible in it.' He wished to eradicate everything from astrology which could not be proved. An astrology purified in this way — *astrologia sana* — would be a part of physics.

The Flemish scientist, physician and philosopher, Jan Baptist van Helmont wanted to test astrology experimentally. He arranged a competition in which a person's time of birth was to be calculated by means of their most important biographical data. Because the results were disappointing, he dismissed birth horoscopy. However, he considered general effects of the constellations as a necessity. He sought to prove the imperative nature of these influences in a treatise with the title, turning the Latin motto on its head, *Astra necessitant non inclinant* (the stars determine, they do not incline).

As the triumphant progress of science began, it was believed that *all* phenomena and events could be understood by means of this science. It was not yet clear which phenomena were suited to this new method and which were not. Many astrologers were completely convinced that the relationships between the human being and the star world could be fully explained by physics. However, when it turned out that the methods of natural science were *not* suitable for all phenomena, the astrologers were faced with a dilemma. If they said that astrology belonged to metaphysics, then it would no longer have held any interest for the scientifically oriented culture of the day. If it were said that astrology was part of natural science, then it would have needed to be able to be proved experimentally. However, this was not successful and so it was increasingly viewed as superstition.

Just at the time when astrology was quickly losing credibility, another achievement was made.

The mathematician Jean-Baptiste Morin was born in the south of France and received his medical degree in Avignon in 1613. In 1630 he was appointed professor of mathematics at the Collège de France. In addition to medicine and mathematics, he had a good reputation in court circles as an astrologer.

He was advisor to Queen Christina of Sweden, Queen Maria of France and the Cardinals Richelieu and Mazarin. Morin's life's work was the *Astrologia Gallica* (1661). He worked for thirty years on this folio volume containing 26 books with a total length of 850 pages. The aim of this work was to introduce a system to the thousands of separate rules for interpreting birth horoscopes. Due to these numerous rules a choice always had to be made out of the many options, giving grounds for arbitrariness. Morin wished to bring order to the countless rules so that a horoscope interpretation could be done methodically and unambiguously. Instead of rules, for which there are always exceptions, he wished to formulate inherent laws. This was the only way, in his opinion, that horoscopy could be made more scientific, and capable of being verified. Although Morin improved the organization of the astrological relationships, he did not make them easier to verify. His work therefore did not make science accept astrology.

Occultism and astrology

Because astrology did not fit into the scientific world view, the triumphant progress of science provided a strong opposing force to astrology. Without a suitable cosmological world view it floated in a vacuum, as it were. It would only have found support from a spiritual picture of the world and mankind, not from a natural scientific one. This support was not possible at the time but had to wait for the end of the dark age. However, the beginnings of a spiritual scientific cosmological world view were already being made during the dark age.

A tremendous achievement was made by Paracelsus, a physician, scientist, philosopher and theologian. His greatest contribution was as a pioneer of modern medicine. But his fame was due in no less measure to his constant search for an understanding of the relationships between the macrocosm and the microcosm. He developed an astrological picture of mankind and the world whose core was formed by the correspondences between the microcosm and macrocosm.

Paracelsus believed empirical research to be essential. He wished to 'read from the book of nature,' to observe the perceptible facts that can be seen 'in the natural light.' But in addition to the findings which can be acquired 'in the natural light' he also believed in those which are to be found 'in the supernatural light.' In addition to empiricism in the world of the senses, there is a higher empiricism which leads to insights into supernatural relationships. His books contain the findings which he discovered on this path.

He called his major work *Astronomia Magna, Philosophia sagax of the great and little world* (1537/38). The word *sagax* is normally translated as astute, but for Paracelsus it is identical with *adeptus*. An adept is one initiated to a greater or lesser degree in the secrets of existence. Paracelsus wished to use the title *Philosophia sagax* to indicate that the book deals with supersensible knowledge.[3]

This shows that Paracelsus was ahead of his time. For human development in general, it was only at the beginning of the light age that it was possible to attain knowledge of the spiritual world through an understanding of the visible world. Paracelsus knew this and described himself as a premature birth.

In Paracelsus' picture of man and the world, the human being is the microcosm, the little world. This reflects the macrocosm in all its details and processes, the big world which comprises the heavens and the earth. The microcosmic human being was born from the macrocosm. Originally, mankind lived in the lap of the gods in paradise. All being was permeated by the life of the stars. Only through the Fall were the microcosmic human being and the macrocosm separated. Since that time humanity experiences the world of the stars as an outer world. But everything outside is also inside. 'The heavens are the human being and the human being is the heavens.'[4] Paracelsus thus renewed an ancient teaching which goes back to Hermes Trismegistus. Although this teaching dates from earliest times, 'it would nevertheless be quite wrong to call Paracelsus an imitator or syncretist. What he puts forward is his very own experience.'

It is not possible to summarize Paracelsus' many-sided world view here. It is typical that, after his death, nothing was said about his work for four hundred years because it was thought to belong to the secret realm of occultism. Even at the start of the twentieth century many saw him as a charlatan or dreamer. It is no coincidence that it was only after the dawn of the light age that Paracelsus' reputation began to be restored. He could not be understood earlier because he was indeed born ahead of his time, an adept initiated in the understanding of nature, 'because he could see the invisible principles at every moment.'[5] His work formed a firm base for a spiritual scientific cosmological view of the world.

The astronomer, Johannes Kepler, was also amongst those who sought a new cosmological picture of the world. It was obvious to him 'that the heavens have an effect on mankind.' The real question was to find out exactly how the influence of the stars worked. An astrology separated from astronomy was unthinkable for Kepler: a science of the stars should include both astronomy and astrology. The spiritual unity of these two should not be torn asunder. But what form should a cosmological picture of the world which included astronomy and astrology take? Kepler was totally misunderstood, just as Paracelsus had been. For many centuries Kepler's three laws were seen as his most important achievement. Only gradually was it discovered, that Kepler himself looked on these laws as only a part of what he considered as his own picture of the cosmos.[6]

Kepler wrote his first work, *Mysterium Cosmographicum* (the secret of the world), at the age of 25. His major work appeared in 1619 under the title *Harmonis Mundi* (the harmony of the world). The two book titles express what he aspired to: the search for the secret of the world and for the harmony of the world.

Kepler compared order in the world to the harmonic relationships in music. He had an inner ear for the rhythms of the music of the spheres. He formulated his famous third planetary law from a consideration of harmonic relationships. This law is described in his book *Harmonis Mundi* as one of many harmonies.

It is indicative of the lack of understanding of Kepler's ideas that his third law was seen as the only worthwhile one in his major work. Kepler himself saw this law as only one of the many proofs of the harmony in the world.

The fourth book of his *Harmonis Mundi* is headed: 'On the harmonic configurations of the rays of the stars seen from the Earth and their influence on weather and other natural phenomena.' It contains wonderful observations of astrological relationships. The Earth reacts to cosmic constellations because the soul of the Earth perceives them. The soul of the Earth reacts to cosmic aspects in a similar way to the consonances and dissonances in music. Kepler experienced the Earth as a living being, an organism with a soul.

His mode of observation made the deficiencies of the materialistic and mechanical picture of the world particularly clear. Only an approach which includes the spiritual realities can do justice to astrological relationships. After discussing the soul of the Earth, the human soul was considered: 'Everything which has been said here about the soul of the Earth can be correspondingly applied to the capacity of the human soul.'[7] Kepler thus introduced completely new spiritual concepts.

Kepler's quest was for an astronomy and astrology renewed through the spirit of music.

His attitude to astrology has been described frequently.[8] Kepler believed that it is only man's character that is cosmically determined. Within this character the human being is free. Kepler's interpretations of the military commander Albrecht von Wallenstein's horoscope still provide grounds for new observations. Ulrike Voltmer recently carried out a thorough analysis in an attempt to reinterpret Kepler's way of working.[9]

Further developments

The directions indicated above show that the encounter with science played an important role in the development of astrology in Europe. The three approaches taken by astrologers can be followed further in the eighteenth and nineteenth centuries.

1. First, there were always astrologers who had visionary talents, and were successful thanks to their gift of prophecy. They were acting 'prescientifically' in the sense that they used little effort for accurate calculations and systematics for interpretation.
2. A very different direction was taken by those who strove for a scientific basis for astrology. Some astrologers of this school refrained from attempting causal explanations. They wished to found a science based on experience which would determine which cosmic-earthly relationships actually exist. In 1896 the Frenchman Paul Choisnard began to make use of statistics and probability theory as a research methodology.[10]
3. A third approach was adopted by those who realized that any quantitatively exact science and any statistical methodology must fail because astrological relationships cannot be explained by natural scientific means alone. They sought a spiritual basis for astrology.

   In the nineteenth century many people foresaw the approach of the light age. The increasingly urgent search for a new spirituality led to the founding of the Theosophical Society (1875) which represented an eastern spiritual heritage. Allan Leo developed an astrological lodge within this society. Soon many astrologers looking for a spiritual path saw theosophy as the ultimate world view for the astrologer. They cultivated an esoteric astrology with three basic theories: first, about the creation of man and the world; secondly, about the parts of the human being (physical body, etheric body, astral body); and thirdly, about karma and reincarnation.

> These teachings were viewed as inseparably connected to astrology. The main representatives of this movement in England were Allan Leo and Sepharial. A later representative of esoteric astrology was Oskar Adler. His work, *Das Testament der Astrologie* was translated into English as *The Testament of Astrology.* Even the title shows that it deals with something inherited from earlier times.

The three directions mentioned here and mixtures of these continued to exist until a new approach to star wisdom was possible at the dawn of the light age.

15. Astrology and Anthroposophy

After the end of the dark age conscious access to the spiritual world became possible again. At the beginning of the twentieth century Rudolf Steiner began to develop his science of the spirit which he called anthroposophy.

The relationship of anthroposophy and astrology is often questioned: what does anthroposophy have to say about astrology? The reason for this question is the fact that anthroposophy has proved very fruitful in some fields such as medicine, education, agriculture, the arts and so on. This gives rise to the question of how anthroposophy can benefit astrology. Is the latter enriched by anthroposophy and if so, how?

This question will be explored here. Because the word 'astrology' so readily brings to mind the form currently in existence, I prefer the expression 'star wisdom' as a general term for what has taken on such differing forms over the course of history. This leaves open the possibility that anthroposophy will give rise to completely new forms of star wisdom.

What is anthroposophy's relationship to star wisdom?

Looking at the history of the development of anthroposophy it is immediately apparent that the two are closely connected. What is the being of anthroposophy? It was not invented by human beings but inspired from the spiritual world. Anthroposophy would not exist on the earth at all if the spiritual world had not inspired it and continues to do so. Where does this inspiration come from? Who inspires anthroposophy? This inspiration is connected to a real spiritual being, the being Anthroposophia.

Even those who have been familiar with anthroposophy for a long time can be surprised to hear that it is connected to a real spiritual being. This was doubtless also the case for those who took up anthroposophy in the early years of the twentieth century.

Rudolf Steiner used the name 'anthroposophy' for the first time in October 1902, in Berlin in the group called *die Kommenden,* a meeting place for young poets, artists and academics.[1] Steiner regularly attended the Thursday evening meetings of this group and became friends with Ludwig Jacobowski, the group's founder. When in 1900 Jacobowski died at the age of 33, Steiner took over leadership of the group.

Starting in October 1902 he held a course of lectures there entitled *From Zarathustra to Nietzsche. History of human evolution based on the world conception of the orient up to the present, or anthroposophy.* This was the occasion when Rudolf Steiner first publicly used the word anthroposophy.

It was more than ten years later, after the founding of the Anthroposophical Society, that he revealed that anthroposophy was connected to a spiritual being. The first general meeting of this society took place in Berlin from February 3 to 7, 1913. On February 3 Rudolf Steiner spoke there for the first time about the inspirational source of the being Anthroposophia.[2] The historical development of this being was described as follows.

In Greek culture she was worshipped as the divine goddess, Sophia. Later, in the Middle Ages, some philosophers experienced how this spiritual being approached them as the lofty Philosophia, as though in a direct human relationship. This being has since developed further, having 'passed through human beings' so that Sophia has become Anthropo-Sophia. In this lecture Rudolf Steiner does not look at her existence in earlier times. He announced that he was going to give four lectures over the following days which would all deal with the being of anthroposophy.

These four lectures during the first general meeting of the Anthroposophical Society were entitled: *The Mysteries of the East and of Christianity.* What do these four lectures contain?

Surprisingly, the being Anthroposophia is not mentioned at all, but a description is given of the development of the spiritual being worshipped in the Egyptian culture, namely the star goddess, Isis.

Egyptian culture was founded by Hermes Trismegistus. He inaugurated the Hermes mysteries which taught that the sky phenomena were an expression of the will of the gods and could be read like a script. These Hermes mysteries led the pupil to an experience of the lofty star goddess, Isis.

In these lectures Steiner described how, at the height of these mysteries, initiation into the secrets of the world of the stars took place in stages, and how in later times, as consciousness of the spiritual world faded, this initiation could no longer take place in full. The star mysteries had to relinquish a living content. The initiates experienced a feeling of grief and resignation. A renewal of the star wisdom will only become possible in our fifth cultural epoch through a renewed mystery being. It is clear that this is a task for anthroposophy.

So on the occasion of the first general meeting of the Anthroposophical Society, Steiner already spoke about the decline of the star mysteries in ancient Egypt and the renewal of these mysteries through anthroposophy.

It is understandable that he felt obliged to talk about the spiritual being connected to anthroposophy at the founding of the Anthroposophical Society. It is more remarkable that — having announced the lectures about this spiritual being — he then spoke about the lofty star goddess, Isis, and about the evolution of star wisdom. Clearly the development of anthroposophy is intimately connected with the renewal of star wisdom.

This is emphasized by the fact that, at the second general meeting of the Anthroposophical Society, Rudolf Steiner again gave a course of lectures on the connection of mankind with the world of the stars. This course comprised four lectures given in Berlin from January 20 to 23, 1914 under the title *Human and Cosmic Thought.*

The lectures describe how the human being is connected to the twelvefoldness of the zodiac and the sevenfoldness of the planets. Twelve world outlooks and seven world outlook moods are described through examples like Hegel, Schopenhauer, Nietzsche, etc.

It is clearly emphasized that this is not a matter of birth horoscopy but of a spiritual astrology.[3] Nowadays we would describe the content of these lectures as a contribution to spiritual astrology.

No further general meetings took place due to the outbreak of the First World War and after the end of the war a consolidation of the society was needed. The society was refounded in 1923 in a completely new form. During the course of that year regional societies were established in Germany which joined to become the General Anthroposophical Society in Dornach at Christmas. Immediately following the refounding Rudolf Steiner once more referred to the task of renewing star wisdom.

While, after the founding of the Anthroposophical Society in 1913, Steiner had spoken about the decline of a living star wisdom in the ancient mysteries, he now described a 'sacrifice of the star knowledge' carried out consciously by human beings, a ritual which took place in the second half of the fifteenth century. This has already been mentioned in Chapter 13.

> Men stood before a kind of altar and said: 'We now resolve to feel responsible not only for ourselves and our community, or our nation, or the people of our time; we resolve to feel responsible for all men who have ever lived on earth, to feel that we belong to the whole of mankind ... In order that man ... may be able to find in freedom of will what Gods have tried to find for him and with him in earlier times, let the higher knowledge be offered up for a period of time.'[4]

The previous lectures described the deeds of the three higher hierarchies in the evolutionary process:

the first hierarchy (Seraphim, Cherubim, Thrones)
the second hierarchy (Kyriotetes, Dynameis, Exousiai)
the third hierarchy (Archai, Archangels, Angels).

These describe how, since the beginning of creation, mankind had been destined to create a fourth hierarchy in addition to the three existing ones. The fourth hierarchy, that of human beings, will become the bearer of freedom. This faculty to be acquired was the reason for the Fall into sin, a separation from the spiritual world, something akin to deserting the rank of the fourth hierarchy.[5] When the 'sacrifice of star knowledge' — consciously, out of insight into the requirements of the development of freedom — was solemnly carried out in a ritual, those gathered for this purpose said, 'We feel that mankind has deserted the rank of the fourth hierarchy and has descended too deeply into matter [for the Fall was understood in this sense] and in order that man may be able to return to the rank of the fourth hierarchy, may be able to find in freedom of will what Gods have tried to find for him and with him in earlier times, let the higher knowledge be offered up for a period of time.'

This 'period of time' lasted until a new relationship to the spiritual world was possible through anthroposophy at the end of the dark age.

At key points in the development of the Anthroposophical Society Steiner repeatedly spoke about the renewal of star wisdom. We can infer from this that Rudolf Steiner considered the birth of anthroposophy to be closely connected with a new birth of the star wisdom.

In answer to the question as to how anthroposophy can enrich astrology it can now be stated that anthroposophy itself intends to form the beginning of a renewal of star wisdom.

This emphasis on the decline of the old star wisdom and the sacrifice of star knowledge in the fifteenth century reinforces the need for the new star wisdom to have a totally different character to what existed in the past. The basis of anthroposophy will give birth to something completely new which will only be able to arise on this foundation.

This should naturally not be taken as a criticism of what exists today as astrology in its many forms and variations. The relationship of this renewal of star wisdom to present-day astrology will be examined in what follows, but first the nature of this renewal will be considered more closely.

The character of the new beginning of star wisdom

As mentioned, at the first general meeting of the Anthroposophical Society the development of star wisdom from the third cultural epoch up to our fifth epoch was described. The question as to *what* anthroposophy can contribute to the foundation of a new star wisdom is, however, also given an important answer in these lectures. The content of these lectures will be described in summary here, in as far as it concerns this question. Naturally this summary is no replacement for reading the lectures.

The lectures of February 5 and 7, 1913 describe in detail the experiences that occurred during the Hermes initiation in ancient Egypt. The soul was raised into higher worlds. Removed from the body, it lived in a world of spiritual deeds and beings. It saw the powers which acted from cosmic worlds into the world of the senses, into the various realms of nature. Looking back at the physical sheaths, it came to know those beings which worked on the creation of the physical and etheric bodies in particular. The experience of how cosmic powers and cosmic beings work on the development of these bodies filled the soul with the deepest satisfaction and bliss.

However, if spiritual researchers look upon the human physical and etheric bodies today, they no longer experience satisfaction and bliss, but are filled with deep concern and uneasiness. Something resembling nerves, but finer than nerves, can be seen running through these bodies. Something has become incorporated into present-day man which appears like dead parts, like a dead inanimate substance to the occult view.

The cause of this is that the star powers, which previously worked to develop the physical and etheric bodies, are no longer able to help build the human body.

In earlier times the human being looking up to the skies saw not only physical stars but felt the stars to be inhabited by spiritual beings. These impressions had a creative effect on the physical and etheric bodies of the human being. By looking up to the expanse of the stars, man had a part in the spiritual powers of the stars.

Nowadays we have a materialistic view of the world. The material view of the cosmos yields very different impressions. These leave a part of the physical and etheric bodies dead, the human being carries dead parts, inanimate 'inclusions' within himself.

If nothing further were to enter, if human beings were to continue to live with a purely materialistic science, then they would degenerate further and further because their souls would no longer receive the forces which contribute to the development of the physical and etheric bodies. This is how Rudolf Steiner described the impression of present-day mankind which fills the initiate with deep concern.

Human beings therefore contain something which is outside their control. Luciferic and Ahrimanic forces can work particularly effectively in these 'dead realms.' This is the reason why so many people have the experience of being in a dilemma nowadays. 'Two souls alas! are dwelling in my breast; And each is fain to leave its brother.' These words from Goethe's Faust sum up much of modern man's experience. The modern path of initiation has the task of overcoming the unconscious dead forces of the soul and body through imbuing the consciousness soul with spiritual knowledge.

'Hence for anyone who looks into these deeper forces of human evolution, everything that can live in the soul must be permeated by a spiritual comprehension of the world.' The insights of anthroposophy must, unlike all ancient mystery knowledge, also be able to be understood by everyone, because the dead forces of the soul and body can only be overcome 'with a knowledge that has been understood and grasped spiritually, not a knowledge built up on authority.'[6]

This is how Rudolf Steiner described the tasks of anthroposophy at the first general meeting of the Anthroposophical Society. In relation to the renewal of star wisdom he did *not* speak of new insights but of a new relationship of mankind to the world of the stars. An understanding of anthroposophy will be able to overcome what is dead and inanimate in the soul and body and heal the division which characterizes modern man. This will enable mankind to regain a relationship to the spiritual forces of the stars. The lost relationship to the world of the stars will be restored.

The contribution of anthroposophy highlighted here is not a new understanding of the star world but the creation of a new relationship to the spiritual forces of the stars.

Naturally this new relationship to the world of the stars will also be accompanied by a renewal of the ideas in astrology. This new relationship of mankind to the star world will now be looked at in more detail.

16. A New Relationship Between Man and the World of the Stars

What form will the new relationship of man and the world of the stars take? In 1914 Rudolf Steiner spoke of an important law which states that the seven post-Atlantean cultural epochs display a mirror image relationship. The cultural development impulse which existed in the first (ancient Indian) cultural epoch will appear again in a new form in the seventh cultural epoch. The impulse which existed in the second (ancient Persian) epoch will appear in a new form in the sixth epoch. Our fifth epoch will see the metamorphosis of what existed in the third cultural epoch.

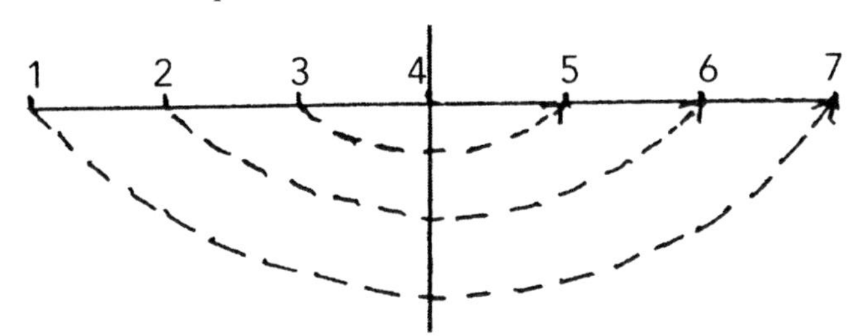

This law contains an important indication of the new element which will arise in our epoch. In the third cultural epoch, star wisdom existed in the form of a *star religion*. The relationship to the world of the stars was based on a real spiritual world inhabited by star gods. In the fourth cultural epoch development of *birth horoscopy* took place. This was related to human life on the earth and aimed to acquire insight into individual human lives with the help of the stars.

The law of reflection shows that the new star wisdom of our epoch — as a mirror of the third epoch — will again be concerned with a real spiritual world. This will not be a metamorphosis of birth horoscopy that has a *unique* position in the fourth epoch. We need to be prepared for the fact that the new star wisdom of our cultural epoch will be something quite different from the study of birth horoscopes.

When explaining the law of reflection, Rudolf Steiner mentioned a research result which only became clear to him after many years, this being that the reflection signifies a Christianizing of what was there earlier. What he actually said was that what will arise in our cultural epoch will be 'a resurrection of the astrology of the third post-Atlantean epoch, but permeated now with the Christ impulse.'[1] In our cultural epoch the star wisdom will therefore flourish in a form permeated by Christ.

This gives rise to the question of what form an astrology permeated by Christ might take? Might the beginnings of this already exist and what would characterize this form of astrology? What is the relationship of astrology to the Christian faith nowadays?

Astrology and Christian faith

Interest in the relationship of astrology and Christian faith has grown significantly in recent times. A series of publications have appeared which address the question of whether astrology is acceptable to the Christian Church and its faith.[2]

These publications represent very varied viewpoints. On the one hand the incompatibility of astrology and Christian faith is clearly established by means of philosophical arguments. Consider, for example, the Roman Catholic church's catechism published in 1992 as a guiding principle for conduct in the twenty-first century:

> All forms of divination are to be rejected: recourse to Satan or demons, conjuring up the dead or other practices falsely supposed to 'unveil' the future. Consulting horoscopes, astrology, palm reading, interpretation of

> omens and lots, the phenomena of clairvoyance, and recourse to mediums all conceal a desire for power over time, history, and, in the last analysis, other human beings, as well as a wish to conciliate hidden powers. They contradict the honor, respect, and loving fear that we owe to God alone.[3]

However, other writings show that both Hindus, Buddhists and Shintoists as well as many diverse new age organizations all practice or can practice the same astrological methods. This indicates that the approach of astrology is philosophically neutral. It is therefore completely acceptable for the Christian faith. These two viewpoints are diametrically opposed nowadays.

When seeking a Christianizing of astrology it must be realized that these two viewpoints do not lead to this goal, because assimilating a philosophically neutral astrological methodology through Christian faith naturally does not bring about a Christianization. But neither does a rejection of astrology by the Christian church achieve this aim.

The significance of the publications in question cannot be overestimated, however, because they have made an important contribution to clarifying opinions. If the two viewpoints are given serious consideration, it becomes apparent that they form an irreconcilable contradiction. Reconciliation of astrology and Christian faith will be impossible as long as they confront each other as two totally separate realities. One speaks about an astrology for which it is basically of no importance whether Christ lived or not. Christ's life on earth has changed nothing for astrology. The other talks of a conception of Christ which is totally unconcerned about what is thought of the world of the stars.

How can a real bridge be built between the world of the stars and Christian faith? Anthroposophy has a clear answer to this question. This bridge can only be built when it is recognized that Christ is a cosmic being. He descended from the cosmos and entered Jesus of Nazareth at the baptism in the Jordan. For three years — between the baptism in the Jordan and the crucifixion

— a cosmic being lived in a human body on earth.

How did the cosmic character of Christ reveal itself? Rudolf Steiner described this in the book *The Spiritual Guidance of Man and Humanity:*

> During the time that Jesus of Nazareth pursued his ministry and journeys as Christ-Jesus in Palestine in the last three years of his life — from the age of thirty to thirty-three — the entire cosmic Christ-being continued to work in him.

This was shown by the fact that he did not take a single step without the cosmic forces working into him.

> The being who walked the earth in those years certainly looked like any other human being. But the forces working in him were the cosmic forces coming from the sun and the stars; they directed his body ... This is why the constellations are so often alluded in the gospel descriptions of Jesus' activities. For example, in the Gospel of St John the time when Christ finds his first disciples is 'about the tenth hour' (John 1:39). In this fact the spirit of the entire cosmos expressed itself in a way appropriate to the appointed moment.[4]

Christ therefore expressed the *current* constellations which were in the sky. He did *not* represent his birth constellation. This is something to bear in mind.

He represented the current star constellations, *not* because he was dependent on the cosmos, but because he was a bearer of cosmic forces. The 'spirit of the whole cosmos' lived in him.

The insight that the spirit of the whole cosmos descended to earth in Christ is of fundamental importance for a renewal of star wisdom in our cultural epoch, for only this insight enables a real bridge to be built between the world of the stars and Christian faith. In this connection it is important that the Christianization of astrology which must occur in our cultural epoch will only be possible if Christianity develops into a *cosmic Christianity.* This further development of Christianity is enduringly connected to a Christianizing of astrology.

Cosmic Christianity

Rudolf Steiner stressed the necessity of recognizing the cosmic significance of the Christ. What we call 'Christianity' nowadays is not yet 'true Christianity': it is merely a shadow of it, a reflection.

Christianity is mostly viewed as a doctrine, but this does not grasp its essential nature. The essence of Christianity is not a doctrine but the events that took place: Christ did not introduce a doctrine, but performed a deed, a deed connected to the evolution of mankind. This reality has scarcely started to enter human consciousness. All the thoughts of the church fathers and the councils in the past were insufficient for such an understanding. While we can admire the tremendous mental effort which was expended in earlier centuries, reason alone is inadequate to understand the mystery of Golgotha. If the development of Christianity had been dependent on human understanding then Christianity would long since have disappeared from the earth. Christianity did not spread because it was understood. It spread because of something else altogether. Those who spread Christianity, the apostles, were simple people. But they were inspired by what they saw, they were enthralled by what they heard, they were seized by enthusiasm. Did the Crusaders understand Christianity? No, they were seized by it. It was inspiration, enthusiasm which was responsible for the spread of Christianity.

Nevertheless, nowadays we need to take the step to an understanding of Christianity. Why? Up until the nineteenth century the Christ impulse could work in human beings even if it was not understood. Since that time this has become increasingly difficult on account of materialism. Now we must progress to understanding, otherwise Christianity will disappear. Christianity has no future without an understanding of the being of Christ. The step to an understanding of the cosmic Christ must now be made. The spirit of the cosmos connected himself to mankind and this has enabled mankind to have a completely new relationship to the world of the stars.

The new relationship between man and the world of the stars

What is the nature of the new relationship to the star world which has arisen due to the mystery of Golgotha? Christ brought the power through which humanity can find the way back to the spiritual world. Above all, since that time the human being can find his true self.

Every person has what can be called their true self: their better self or their higher self. What we usually call our 'self' is not our true self. When someone says, 'My name is John, I am English and live in London,' then it is not their true self that is speaking. Because this self is unable to say these things about itself. The true self goes through many incarnations: it is embodied differently in different earth lives.

In the era of the consciousness soul in which we currently live we have become true citizens of the earth. We have become at home on the earth. In this process the awareness of the true self has been lost to mankind. In the present day many people live in darkness as regards their true self, something which is apparent in their struggle with life's questions. What shall I do with my life? Am I on the right path? Should I do something completely different from what I'm doing at present? What is the real purpose of my life? What kind of life should I lead? Where can I find what I ought to do?

These kind of questions disturb our thoughts nowadays. This struggle with the questions presented by life shows how people wrestle with their relationship to the true self. These struggles in life belong to our time, because in the era of the consciousness soul the true self must be born in the soul.

This true human self has its home in the world of the stars. After death the human being travels through the spiritual world, through the planetary spheres. There he finds his true self. This guides him through the spiritual world of the stars, through the planetary spheres. The true human self is a star self. It is literally our guiding star.

The purpose of life's struggles is that they encourage the

human being to find his true self. Such trials will become ever greater in the coming centuries. Dissatisfaction with our own lives will continue to grow.

Rudolf Steiner described how the human being will in future feel himself to be a cosmic being.

> As though with outstretched arms he will demand a solution to the riddle of his cosmic being. This is what will come about in the coming decades, that man will eagerly ask, 'Who will unravel the mystery of my nature for me as a cosmic being? All that I can establish on earth, all that the earth can give me, all that I can get from natural science which is valued so highly nowadays, only solves the mystery of my earth being and leaves the real being of man as an unsolved riddle. I know that I am a cosmic, heavenly being: who will solve the riddle of my heavenly being?'[5]

Man thus becomes a seeker for his star self.

Because the spirit of the cosmos became man and went through death as a human being, we can now carry the fruits of our earthly struggles, our search for the star self through death into the spiritual world. Every human being nowadays struggles with life's questions. This is a necessity in our time when the self is awakening in the soul. Through this struggle we gain new qualities in life and these we can carry through the gate of death into the spiritual world. This is the fundamental change which has arisen in our relationship to the spiritual world of the stars: at the moment of death we become *contributors* towards the spiritual world. Our relationship to the cosmos becomes a *giving* relationship.

The moment of death is a deeply moving, shocking one for human beings. The physical body is laid aside. The first thing which we experience after death is a panorama of our life. What in life has taken place as a sequence of events is there all at once. A whole tableau of the life which has come to an end appears in a wealth of pictures.

This life tableau is woven into the stars at the moment of

death. The aspects, the groupings of the stars are reflected in it. The life panorama and the star grouping at the moment of death resonate together.

A spiritual birth takes place, a birth into the spiritual world. Just as the grouping at the moment of birth on earth expresses the experiences in the prebirth spiritual world, so the grouping at the moment of death is a summing-up of the life which has finished. It is a summary in cosmic language, in cosmic writing.

This forms a starting point for a renewal of star wisdom in relation to mankind. Rudolf Steiner suggested that, instead of looking at the aspects of the stars at the moment of birth in the physical world, we should look at the aspects of stars at the moment when a human being is born into the spiritual world.

> Investigations are often made — unfortunately not always with the necessary respect and dignity, but out of egoistic reasons — into the starry constellations [groupings] prevailing at birth. Much less selfish and much more beautiful would be a horoscope, a planetary horoscope for the moment of death.[6]

This statement by Steiner opens up great possibilities. It sets us the task of looking at a person's death constellation instead of their birth constellation. It is something revolutionary which never happened in the past. Although in earlier times the person who had died was followed on their way through the world of the stars in their life after death, the life they had lived on earth was never considered in connection with their death constellation. This has only been possible since Christ as a cosmic being became man and went through death as a human being. The result of this deed is that the human being can now carry the fruit of his life on earth through death. This fact is valid for *all* mankind, because Christ went through death for the whole of humanity.

Contemplating the star groupings of a spiritual birth

Contemplating the star constellation of a spiritual birth requires a completely different inner attitude towards the world of the stars than we are used to, a totally different moral attitude. 'Respect and devotion' are what Rudolf Steiner calls the qualities required for this path: 'if the necessary respect and devotion were applied ...'

When mention is made nowadays of this possibility of looking at the star constellation of a spiritual birth it is often said, 'What use is that? The person in question is already dead, nothing more can be done for them.'

But this is precisely the point! The life of the person concerned has taken shape. We can view his struggles on earth. Precisely because we know about this person's life on earth, the aspects of his spiritual birth can begin to 'speak.' The star groupings can express something in the light of the life which has been accomplished.

This reflects a significant change of direction from earlier times. Previously the birth aspects were studied in order to understand the person. What is new, is that it is not observation of the heavens which leads to an understanding of the person, but the cosmos is viewed through the events of a person's life. Knowledge is gained of the cosmos.

It is this change of direction which requires selflessness. Every form of egoism forms an obstacle. To undertake this research requires not only respect but also unconditional love for the stars, love for the world of the stars.

For the future of star wisdom it is very important that we learn to see the aspects of a spiritual birth as a picture of the human being. This requires that human beings learn to view the heavens *pictorially.* This pictorial way of seeing sky phenomena was present in earlier times but has been lost. Nowadays we live with spatial images and view sky phenomena spatially. We say, 'Oh, how far away the stars are! The moon is relatively close; astronauts went there first.'

Naturally there is nothing wrong with looking at the sky in this way. It is justified for earthly reality, but if human beings wish to approach the spirit, then they need to learn to see heavenly phenomena pictorially.

For example:

— Are the planets, Sun and Moon close together in the sky as though in a cluster, or are they scattered loosely about?
— Are the planets all *above* the horizon or all *below* it?
— Are they rising or setting?

What appears in the skies can be taken as an expression of the human being. This requires practice in observing the skies. The heavenly phenomena must be familiar, not only in an outer sense but also in an inner one.

The starry groupings of a spiritual birth are an 'open secret,' that is, although everyone can see the constellation, a true 'seeing' has to be learned. This belongs to the fundamentals of the new star wisdom.

17. Fundamentals of a Spiritual Star Wisdom

Despite being so tied to the earth, the human soul has a deep inner feeling for its connection to the cosmos. Those who seek the connection of mankind to the world of the stars out of this feeling can find a possible answer in what exists in our culture as astrology. Astrology uses the signs of the zodiac and the planets in an interesting symbolic language and comes to statements relating to people. Although astrology makes many interesting statements, when we seek a scientific or even a clear basis for these statements, it cannot provide an answer. For astrology comes from a time before modern science came into existence. It has been unable to contribute anything to the development of science since the sixteenth century and science for its part could not be reconciled to the astrological tradition. In past centuries it has not been possible to build a scientific foundation for the application of astrology.

It is obvious to the spiritual view that the human being is more than merely a creature of nature. Pure natural science, however amazing it may be, can never fathom the relationship of the human being to the world of the stars. This requires a science of the spirit. The basis of a spiritual star wisdom is given by Rudolf Steiner in *Esoteric Science.* This work describes how, in the course of a long evolution, the cosmos, earth and mankind have developed in relation to one another. The human being and the cosmos are inseparably connected. The microcosm and macrocosm belong together like two brothers. *Esoteric Science* is the seed of a new science of the relationship of man and the world of the stars. The development of this seed still needs a great deal of time and energy. Willi Sucher has made a start on this and his work forms the basis of the statements which follow.

What will be developed with the help of anthroposophy is not traditional astrology but a science which is appropriate for our present time. During human evolution human beings had different kinds of awareness at different times. Our present day requires other kinds of knowledge and new viewpoints than those expressed by traditional astrology, which originates from times when people still possessed clairvoyant faculties. This visionary consciousness has been lost in the course of time. Parallel to this, however, new faculties of perception and thinking developed. For obvious reasons, traditional astrology is no longer comprehensible for modern consciousness. We now have to start from the cognitive powers of our time: exact perception and thinking, and move on to developing them further into higher cognitive faculties: imagination, inspiration and intuition.[1] Steps in this direction were made by Willi Sucher.

What can we do?

What can we do to contribute to the development of a new star wisdom? The first step is to become aware of our own position within the historical development of star wisdom: where do we stand in the developmental process of the way in which human beings experience the relationship of man and the world of the stars?

We live in the age of space travel. This gives the impression not only that the cosmos is a realm which can be crossed by space-ships, but that this is the only truth. We view the sky as a physical realm subject only to physical laws. This science of the spatial world view is spread in a popular form. Every educated person nowadays knows that the stars are far away. Their distances are measured in light years; that is, how many years the light from a star travels (at a speed of 300,000 km per second) until it enters our eye. Space probes have been sent to Jupiter and Venus. Great discoveries have been made, for instance there are craters, or farra, on Venus, so it can be concluded that Venus is volcanic.

These scientific ideas — produced with the aid of modern measuring methods — are made available to people in a simple form nowadays. And these ideas are very powerful. Their effect is twofold.

First they have the effect that the heavens are no longer really 'heaven,' no longer a spiritual realm where spiritual beings actually exists, where those not yet born and those who have died dwell. A few hundred years ago the heavens were still the home of the gods, not a place for investigating the chemical composition of the stars and where their distance can be measured in light years. In the course of only a few hundred years the cosmos has become something material, physical to our eyes. Understanding of the spiritual cosmos has faded.

A second consequence is the alienation of modern man from pure observation of the sky. How difficult it is to see the heavens purely as a picture and not spatially. When we look at the starry sky, scientific ideas immediately push between us and the phenomena, 'Oh, how incredibly far away the stars are!' We completely forget that the sky initially reveals itself to us as a picture. To our observation it is only a picture and has a picture character. We do not see any depth. Anyone who is involved with the phenomena of the starry sky discovers that there is a gulf between the scientific ideas and what can be seen by pure observation.

A modern astronomy book points out that the rising and setting of the Sun and planets is only apparent: 'in reality' the Earth turns on its axis. Do the planets follow looping movements in the sky? They only appear to do so. Because the Copernican view of the world clearly shows that the planets rotate in circular paths around the Sun. The looping movement is only an appearance, not reality. Constellations? Stars forming pictures? The appearance is deceptive, because the individual stars in a 'constellation' are not connected at all. They are located at very different distances away from us. The modern creed is therefore: *what can be seen with the naked eye is not reality, but only appearance.* Pure sense perception is of no importance for modern science. *Only what can be measured and recorded by means of instruments is valid.* The present-day astronomical world view does not describe what people see, only what instruments record.

It is no surprise that the most elementary simple knowledge of sky phenomena has disappeared. Many people are completely lost when they wish to find their way about in the sky at night.

The birth of a new star wisdom requires that the heavens once again become heaven, and that observation of the sky is practised. We shall consider these two tasks in what follows.

The heavens must become heaven again

The knowledge that the heavens are no longer heaven awakens a need in the soul to look at the heavens differently. We can become aware that our spatial conception of the cosmos has arisen from the Copernican world view. Before Copernicus, Ptolemy's world view applied. This world view still talked about the 'spheres.' The Sun and planets moved in their spheres. What was meant by these spheres, for example the Sun sphere?

The first step in answering this question is to ask ourselves: what was meant at that time by the concept 'Sun'? When we speak of the Sun we know what is meant, that is, the ball of gas which we can see in the sky during the day. But in those days if someone had asked, what do you mean when you speak of the Sun, do you mean the spring, summer, autumn or winter sun? These are naturally very different.

What do we mean when we say 'human being'? Do we mean the infant, the school child, the adolescent, the adult or the old person? By 'human being' we mean the totality of these phenomena. Similarly, the Sun sphere comprises the totality of its manifestations. This conception arose from observation and experience of the phenomena. Human beings formed *qualitative* concepts. The way of observing at the time meant that the Ptolemaic picture of the cosmos was not spatial in the modern sense. The spheres were also not thought of spatially, but spiritually. Space travel would have been unthinkable in those days.

This way of looking has disappeared nowadays. Modern astronomy has become totally physical in nature. As mentioned, it bases its picture of the cosmos only on what can be recorded by instruments and not on direct observation. This view gained ascendency around 1600. As long as we adhere only to this, the Copernican picture of the cosmos is irrefutable.

Anthroposophy gives us a different picture of the cosmos. In this world view the human being is intimately bound up with the cosmos. This relationship of the human being to the cosmos becomes clearest through the description of the path which man travels after death, for this is when he enters the spiritual spheres of the planets.

Life between the boundaries of birth and death is only a small part of our whole existence for the spiritual scientific view, for we existed before birth and we will continue to live after death. At death the physical body is laid aside and, soon afterwards, the etheric body. All that the human being is in addition to his body frees itself from the corpse and enters the spiritual supersensible world.

In recent decades many near-death experiences have come to light. These reports agree in many respects. Those concerned describe how they experienced themselves in space outside their body and saw themselves from outside. At this moment their consciousness was filled with pictures which portrayed the most important events of their past life in a complete tableau. This overview of their life was not alarming: in general the facts of their past life were viewed without any judgment.

Anthroposophy describes how all this comes about. The essential being of mankind, his 'I,' lives in three sheaths during life: the physical body, the etheric body and the astral body. At death the human being leaves the physical body. The etheric body (also called the life body) is the bearer of memory. When it disconnects from the physical body at the moment of death, the tableau of memories covering the whole life immediately starts to unfold.

What really happens at death cannot be fully experienced

in near-death experiences because of course these people have returned to life. Those who really die experience how, after about three days, it is no longer possible to keep hold of the life tableau. It spreads out, becomes larger and larger and disappears from the view of the one who has died into the cosmos. Just as the physical body disintegrates and returns to the material world from where it came, so the etheric body also returns to the world where it originated, into the etheric cosmos. After the life tableau has dissolved, the astral body and 'I' pass into a new state of existence. Both travel through the world of the soul which is also called kamaloka where a purification takes place until the astral body can also be laid aside. Only after this time, does the I, the ego, move into the actual spiritual world. The human being lives through this until he can finally turn to a new incarnation. In order to incarnate, the essential being must take on the three sheaths again: the astral, etheric and physical bodies.

This journey of the human being through the world after death is described by anthroposophy in considerable detail.[3] This is possible because the spiritual world which the human being passes through has a particular structure.

When passing through the worlds of soul and spirit, human beings experience themselves as extending into the cosmos. Life after death is passed through in the cosmos, in the planetary spheres, where the human being experiences in sequence the spheres of Moon, Mercury, Venus and Sun (the four regions of the world of soul) and the spheres of Mars, Jupiter and Saturn (the three regions of the spiritual world). In each of these spheres the one who has died has experiences characteristic for that sphere. After what is known as the 'world midnight hour' the 'I' passes through the planetary spheres in the reverse order on the way to a new incarnation on the earth.

The human being therefore spends the larger part of existence in the spiritual world of the stars. *In essence the human being is a celestial being, a cosmic being.* Only if this reality is taken seriously will the heavens be able to be viewed once more as a spiritual realm.

Difficulty is often experienced in matching this anthroposophical view of life after death with the Copernican world view. We must realize that the Copernican world view in our culture is only 450 years old. It arose at the time when people became true citizens of the earth and developed a form of cognition tied to the physical body. Anthroposophy helps us to understand that we can only accept the spatial Copernican world view as truth as long as we live in our physical body between birth and death. As soon as we leave our physical body our consciousness changes and therefore also our view of the cosmos. A spiritual view of the cosmos begins as soon as we leave our physical body, either at the moment of death or on the path to higher knowledge.

The practice of observing the sky

Renewal of the star wisdom will not take place if observation of sky phenomena is neglected. A contemporary star wisdom needs to be founded on the faculties of exact perception and thinking and on their further development into higher cognitive abilities: imagination, inspiration and intuition. The development of a new star wisdom is not something which can be achieved overnight. It will have to be worked on long and hard for progress to be made. But a solid foundation can be made by anyone who tries to observe the positions of the planets daily and visualize their movements over a longer period of time.

It is of great help when learning the sky phenomena to visualize the position of the zodiac in the sky through the course of 24 hours. The constellation of the zodiac describing the highest arc in the sky in the northern hemisphere is Gemini. We can visualize this arc by following the summer Sun which is in this constellation. The constellation of Sagittarius describes the lowest arc in the sky which is shown by the winter Sun. The constellations of Virgo and Pisces follow medium arcs. If we picture this movement we can see a kind of 'dance of the zodiac' over the course of 24 hours (see Figure 2 on page 138).

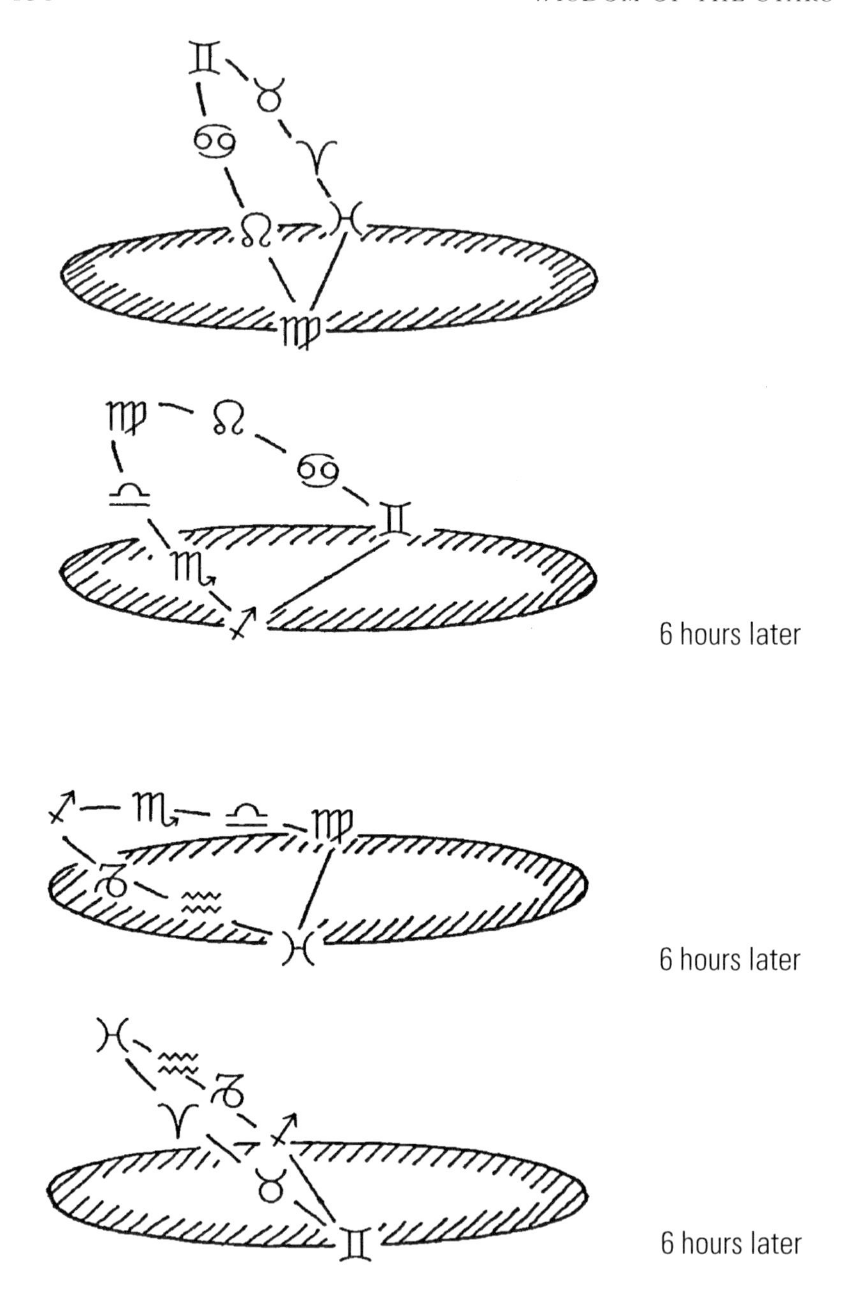

Figure 2. The 'dance of the zodiac' over 24 hours
(From: Elisabeth Mulder, Sonne, Mond und Sterne)

This can also be practised during the day when the stars and planets are not visible. If the location of the planets in the zodiac is known, it is possible to visualize the position of the zodiac and the location of the planets in the sky at any time of the day. If we practise this over an extended period, then our familiarity with the sky will deepen, becoming a real experience.

Starting from our immediate perception, we always find ourselves as the observer in the centre of the phenomena. If we stand under a clear cloudless sky at night, then the cosmos is around us on all sides. We experience the sky as a dome, a hemisphere above us. The stars are visible *above* us. We can observe how they rise in the east and set in the west. We therefore know that the world of the stars is also *below* us, invisible, because they are concealed by the earth. One half of the sky is visible, the other half invisible. The visible and invisible parts are divided by the horizon. We see the horizon as a level plane, the surface of the earth which divides the whole sky into two halves.

All stars and planets follow paths which rise in the east and set in the west, and (in the northern hemisphere) reach their highest point in the south. Looking southwards we can imagine a plane going through the south point and north point and being at right angles to the horizon. This plane divides the sky into two halves, just as the horizon does. Left of this plane all heavenly bodies move upwards, right of it they move downwards.*

If we not only observe these phenomena but also have an inner experience of them, then the space around us becomes qualitatively differentiated. The area *above* the horizon could be called the *'daytime world.'* There we relate to the visible phenomena. Likewise, during the day there are the invisible stars and planets in the daytime world. *Below* the horizon is the non-manifest, with which the human being is not connected in an outer manner but in an inner one. This we shall call the *'nighttime world.'*

* In the southern hemisphere Sun, Moon and stars reach their highest point in the north. It can be an interesting exercise to visualize the movement of the zodiac in the opposite hemisphere.

Just as day and night alternate in human life, so the sky is divided into a 'day half' above the horizon and a 'night half' below the horizon. The upward moving phenomena in the eastern half of the sky are also experienced qualitatively as 'rising,' as a 'beginning.' When day breaks and the Sun rises the day lies before us with many fresh opportunities. The downward movement of the phenomena in the western half of the sky gives us a certain feeling of heaviness. What was still full of potential and opportunity has now been formed, finished, weighed down.

This may sound strange or odd at first. However, it is a tentative attempt to bring the space around us closer to our experience again. A new star wisdom will only be able to come about fully and completely when this feeling for the quality of space is reawakened. This feeling has been lost due to the scientific quantitative perspective which knows no qualitative difference between above and below. Rising and setting have disappeared as realities. In earlier times the qualities of space were still experienced with instinctive faculties which had not been gained consciously. It can be seen as a positive development that this instinctive kind of experience disappeared because through the loss of these innate faculties it became possible for mankind to achieve a free relationship towards the cosmos. Through man's free and conscious endeavours a new way of experiencing the cosmos can arise in the future. This new kind of experience will be essential for a renewal of star wisdom.

The new star wisdom

We have seen that the birth of a new star wisdom will only be possible when the heavens are again actually viewed as 'heaven' i.e. as a spiritual realm with which the human being has a real connection in the life between death and a new birth. It has also been mentioned that the birth of a new star wisdom requires us to practise observation of the sky in such depth that a real *experiential relationship* to the sky phenomena comes about.

When people take up these two tasks this will give rise to an inner change, bringing about a completely new experience of the relationship of mankind to the cosmos. The knowledge that the human being leads an existence in the spiritual world of the stars between death and a new birth changes the way that we view the night sky. The twinkling stars evoke a feeling in the soul of a deep connection to the cosmos. The fact that, at death, man enters the spiritual cosmos, in other words is born into the spiritual world of the stars, is felt to be completely natural.

In the quest for connections between the human being and the world of the stars, it can therefore no longer be considered as real and meaningful to direct attention solely to the human being's earthly moment of birth as is done by present-day astrology. The moment of human birth in the spiritual world and the aspects of the stars associated with this become of interest. A completely new viewpoint appears. Traditional astrology is characterized by a strongly developed interest in the aspects of the stars at the birth of a person in the physical world. The experiences which occur on the path to a new star wisdom, however, awaken an equally natural interest in the constellation of the stars at a person's moment of death, that is, at his birth into the spiritual world.

18. The Stars at a Spiritual Birth

Can the grouping of stars at the moment of spiritual birth express something about the relationship of the human being to the world of the stars? Rudolf Steiner pointed out the importance of this questions.[1] Willi Sucher endeavoured to conduct research in this area.

The nature of this relationship can best be described by using some examples of well-known historical figures. Calculations are necessary to determine aspects from the past, but this need not be an obstacle to us imagining these groupings and bringing them to life in our experience. The aspects at the birth in the spiritual world of Pascal and Michelangelo will be discussed below. A short review of their biographies will first be given followed by observation of the aspects.

Pascal and Michelangelo

Blaise Pascal was a famous seventeenth-century mathematician and philosopher. From childhood onwards his main interests lay in scientific and mathematical topics. His longing for knowledge was linked to a real love of discovery. For instance, he built a calculating machine called a Pascaline. His interests gave him access to academic circles from an early age and he was highly esteemed by his contemporaries. When he was 31 he had a mystical experience, an experience of Christ. For the rest of his life he carried a note about this moving experience around with him. The experience wrought an inner change in him: he entered the monastery of Port Royal near Paris and endeavoured to follow an inner path.

He did not find this easy and his life increasingly became

a struggle with inner doubts until his early death at the age of 39. In the final years of his life he wrote down his thoughts on morality, religion, the inner life of man and the mystery of Jesus. At the end of his life he was beset by inner conflict and it was only after his death that his notes were published and spread his fame.

The life of Michelangelo, the famous sculptor, painter and architect had a very different character to that of the inward-looking life of Pascal. He created huge works in the outer world which can still be seen to this day. Think for instance of the five-metre-high statue of David in Florence and the frescoes in the Sistine Chapel in Rome. There are 340 figures represented on the ceiling on an area of 500 square metres, all of which he painted himself. This was hard work as he had to produce them in a difficult posture, actually lying on a scaffolding. He worked for over thirty years on the tomb of Pope Julius II in Rome.

Michelangelo lived at the centre of public life. He received contracts from kings and popes, sometimes impossible ones which he could barely accomplish. In addition, the contracts were constantly changed along the way, depending on the mood of the patron, often being made and then broken again. Michelangelo was embroiled in lawsuits which lasted for years.

He had to struggle not only with marble and other materials but also with his patrons and with trying circumstances.

It is not difficult to see the polar opposite character of Pascal's inward-directed life and Michelangelo's which was aimed at achievement in the outer world.

Let us now look at the stars of their spiritual births. Blaise Pascal died in Paris on August 19, 1662 (Gregorian calendar) at 1 am.[2] At this moment, both Sun and Moon as well as the classical planets were below the horizon, in the 'nighttime half' of the sky. Michelangelo died on February 18, 1564 (Julian calendar) in Rome at 5 pm.[3] The constellation of his spiritual birth shows the Sun, Moon and all the classical planets above the horizon, in the 'daytime' half of the sky.

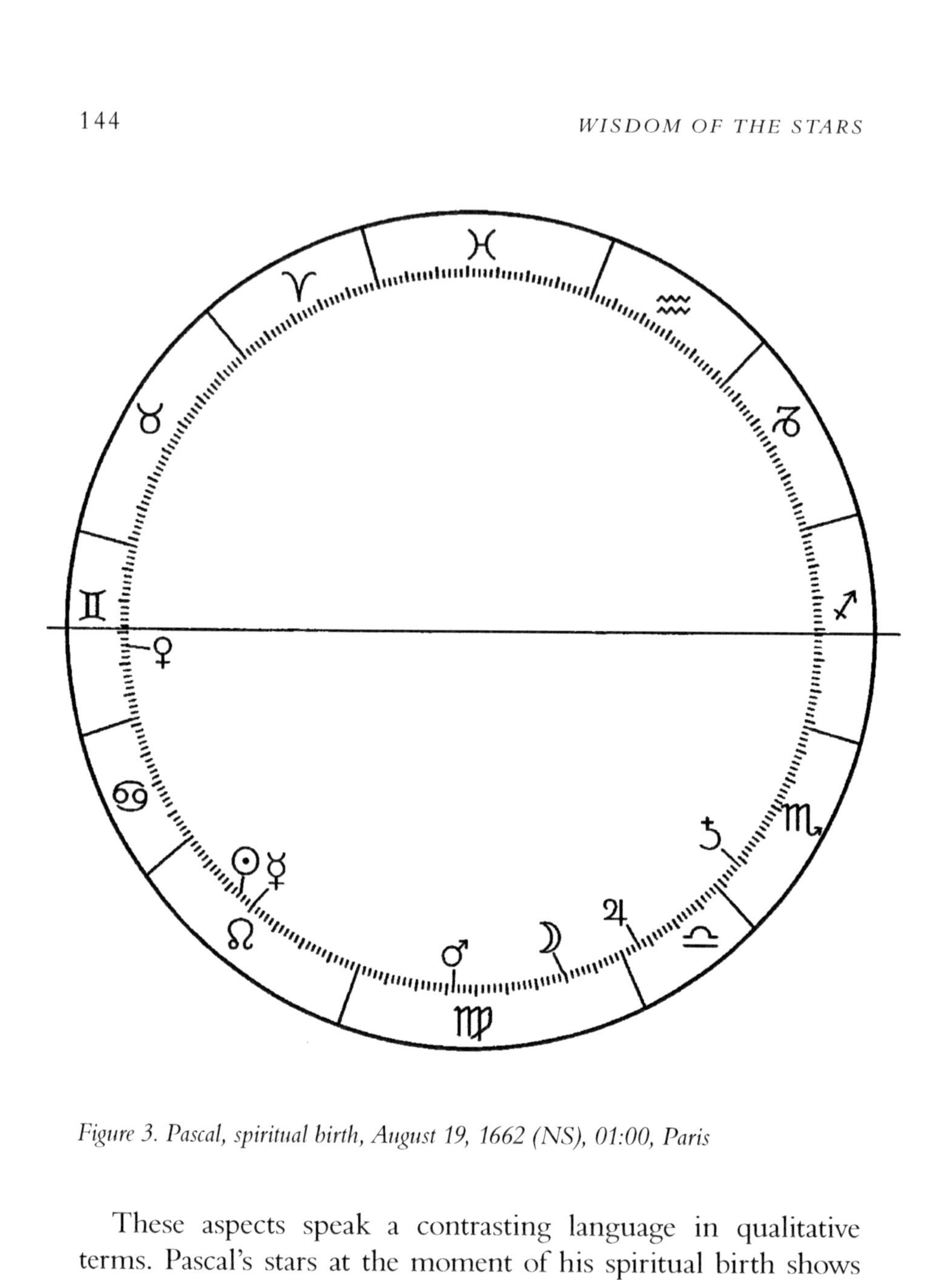

Figure 3. Pascal, spiritual birth, August 19, 1662 (NS), 01:00, Paris

These aspects speak a contrasting language in qualitative terms. Pascal's stars at the moment of his spiritual birth shows a personality with a soul life directed inwards towards the 'nighttime side.' When, after a life which had been lived in public, Michelangelo was born into the world of the stars, a constellation in the sky appeared which was oriented towards the 'daytime side' of the sky, towards life in the public eye. These parallels are truly amazing.

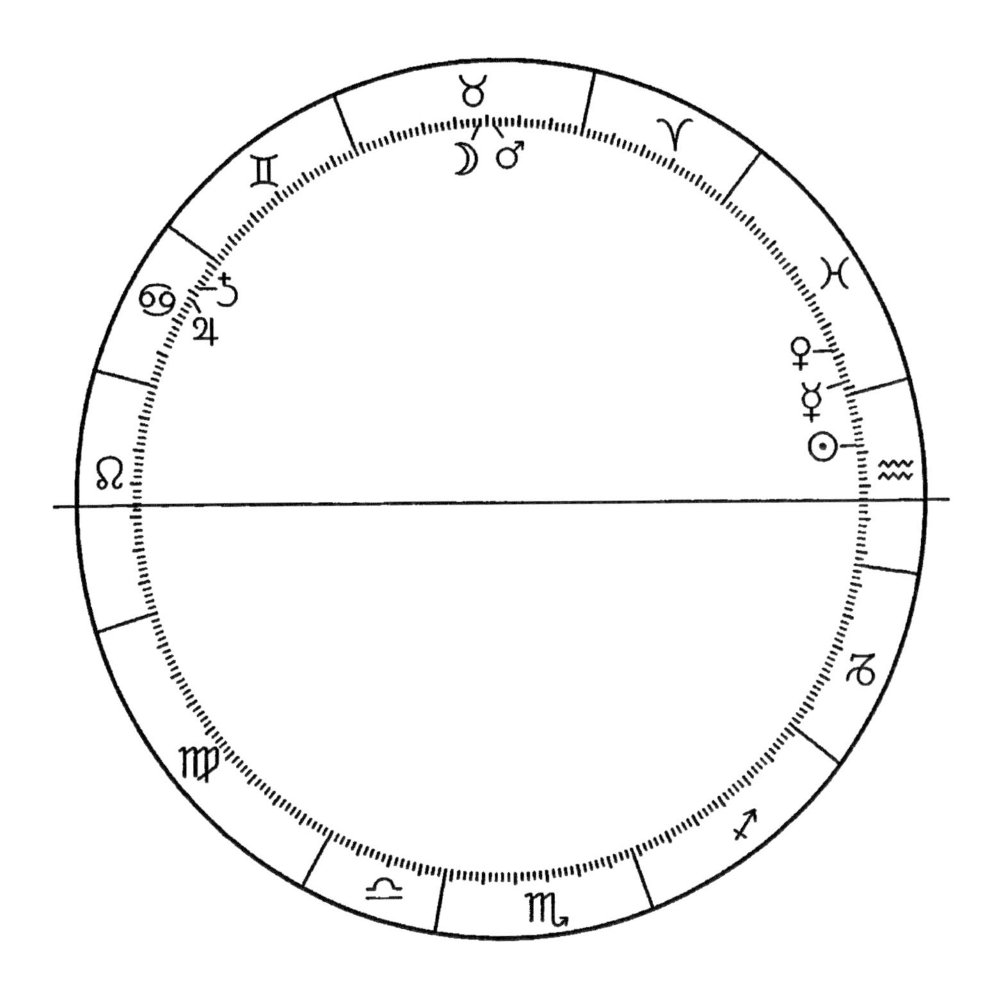

Figure 4. Michelangelo, spiritual birth, February 18, 1564 (OS), 17:00, Rome

It is clear that the biographies of these men express a particular gesture as do the star constellations of their spiritual births, and these two gestures match.

Polar opposite examples were intentionally chosen here to make it clear what is meant by the statement that, at a person's spiritual birth, the sky displays a star constellation which is related to the person in question. Only the classical planets, Sun and Moon are mentioned. Uranus, Neptune and Pluto are not considered because, when reading the star writing, it is best to begin as simply as possible. It is recommended that beginners should limit themselves to what can be seen with the naked eye. Naturally the relationship between the human being and the star world at the moment of their birth in the spiritual world is not always so easy to understand as in the above examples. However, the connection is always visible if the spiritual birth corresponds with the will of the powers of fate.

Blaise Pascal

Let us look at the life of Pascal in more detail. He was born in Clermont-Ferrand in 1623. His mother died in 1626 and his father moved to Paris with the three children in 1631. The young Blaise had a passionate love of mathematics and at only sixteen wrote a paper on conic sections. In his twenties he lived a worldly life, frequenting the salons of fashionable people. It is recorded that he 'had the appearance of a courtier and behaved as such.' 'He lived frivolously, was constantly in the company of beautiful women and enjoyed life.' This is the 'worldly period,' during which he was filled with a love for the world and for life.

His conversion took place in 1654 (he was then 31). This was the year of grace, as he called it. One November night he had an experience of Christ which turned his life completely upside down. He recorded the memory of this experience in his famous Memorial. He sewed the parchment with the words into the lining of his coat and always carried them around with him. The beginning of this Memorial reads:

> YEAR OF GRACE 1654
>
> Monday November 23, day of Saint Clement, pope and martyr and others in the martyrology.
>
> Eve of the day of Saint Chrysogonus, martyr, and others. From around half past ten in the evening until around half an hour after midnight.
>
> FIRE

After this experience Pascal withdrew to a monastery. There his inner work increased.

When he was 34, in addition to other scientific work, he formulated a theory on the game of roulette which challenged the mathematicians of Europe to a contest. He also began his *Apology for Christianity,* an apology and polemic against the Jesuits. Pascal's argumentative nature was displayed here to the highest degree.

However, eighteen months later in 1659 his energies were exhausted. He fell into a state of complete collapse. Physically spent, he was no longer able to carry out any regular work.

Then, two years before his death, he began to write down his thoughts on small slips of paper. These notes were later collected and arranged, appearing eight years after his death as his most famous work, *Pensées,* the fruits of the last two years of his life.

As already mentioned, at the moment of death the human being experiences a tableau of memories due to the release of his etheric body. This shows him his past life in living pictures over the course of three days. It is important to note that, for the relationship of the human being to the world of the stars, this life tableau is in harmony with the star constellation at the moment of their spiritual birth in the world of the stars. As mentioned previously, Rudolf Steiner made reference to this fact. Can we find confirmation of this indication?.

Let us try to bring Pascal's biography to life like a journey. Fairy tales often describe how the central figure passes through different stages of experience on the journey of life. We can also try to visualize Pascal's life in this qualitative pictorial way.

If we place ourselves in Pascal's biography in the right way, then the following stages appear:

— worldly period: love of the world and life;
— year of grace: experience of Christ;
— awakening of his argumentative nature: polemic;
— physical exhaustion;
— writing down his ideas *(Pensées).*

If we now visualize the planetary groupings during his life we find a connection. We need to look at the path of Saturn through the zodiac. Saturn passes through the zodiac in about thirty years. Saturn was in Cancer at Pascal's birth in 1623. It passed through almost the whole zodiac as far as the constellation of Gemini by 1650/51. If we look at the course of Saturn during Pascal's life we find the following relationships.

— When Pascal was going through his worldly period (1650/51), filled with love for the world and for life, Saturn was in the position where later, at the moment of death, Venus — originally the goddess of beauty and love — stood. It is as though Venus was recalling this time.
— In the year of grace Saturn was in the position where later, in the death grouping, Sun and Mercury — originally the god of transformation — were. These two recall the year of his experience of Christ and the inner transformation.
— In 1657 Saturn was in the position where later, in the death grouping, Mars was located. Thus the position of Mars (the Roman god of war) indicated that time in Pascal's life when his argumentative nature awoke.
— When Saturn was at the position where later, in the moment of death, the Moon (representative of reproductive and life forces) stood, Pascal's life forces declined to a point of total exhaustion.
— In 1660 Pascal began to write down his ideas. At this time Saturn was in the position where later, in the death groupings, Jupiter (representative of wisdom) stood.

This shows an astonishing connection between the stages in Pascal's life and the cosmic planetary aspects at the moment of his death. It is as though his biography was expressed in this constellation.

The central role played by Saturn in this is striking. Anthroposophy shows that Saturn represents the memory of the planetary system. Rudolf Steiner described the beings connected to our planetary system. The sphere of Mars is inhabited by

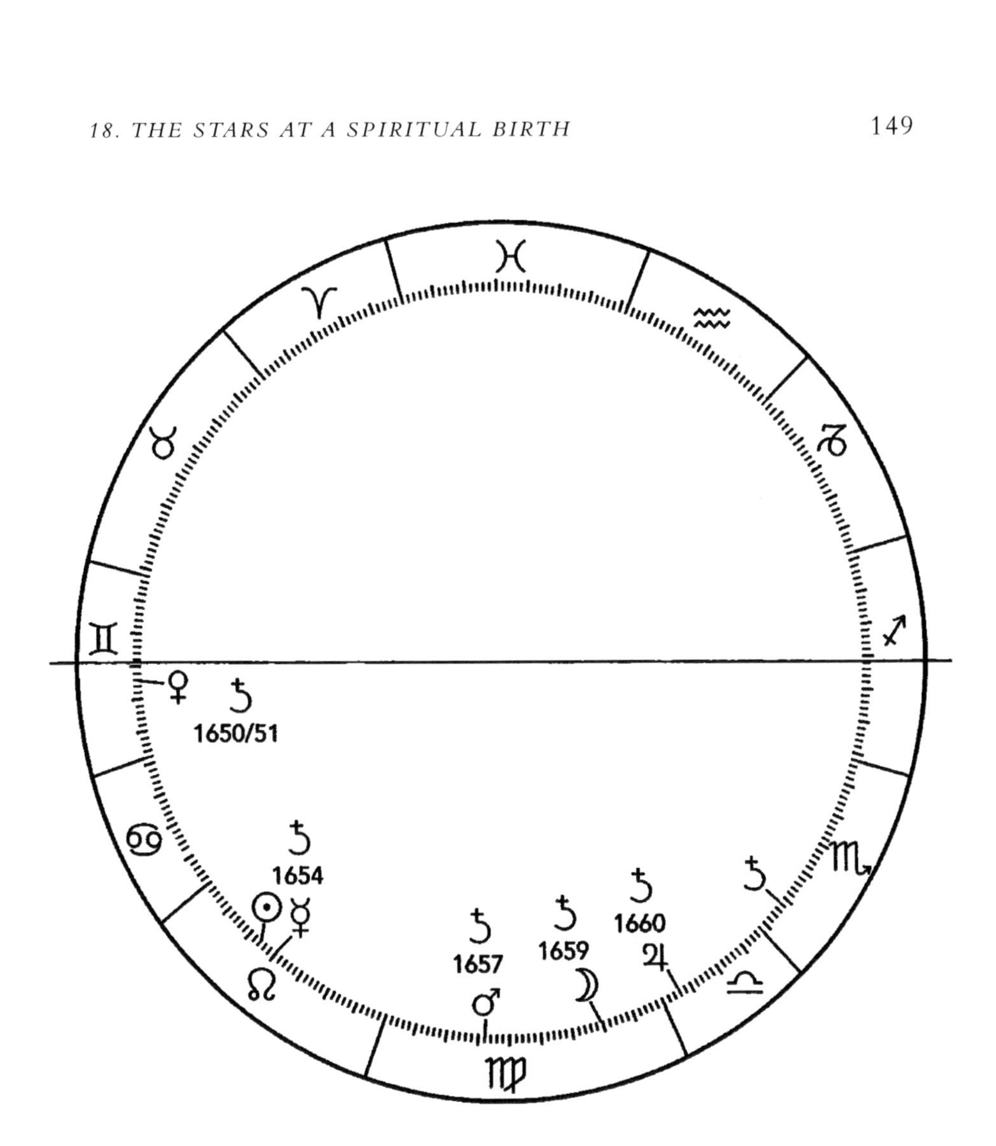

Figure 5. Pascal, spiritual birth, August 19, 1662 (NS), 01:00, Paris

beings who give mankind the ability to speak while the Jupiter beings are bearers of wisdom-filled thoughts. The sphere of Saturn is inhabited by spiritual beings who preserve the memory of the past. The Saturn beings absorb everything that happens, preserve it and only speak of past events. They are the keepers of memory in the cosmos. 'When first considered from a cosmic viewpoint, Saturn is something like the wandering memory of our planetary system.'[4] This explains why Saturn is the planet which has an important role as preserver of the past in the constellation of a spiritual birth.

The astonishing connection between the stages in Pascal's life and the stars at the moment of his death raises the question of how this comes about. Did the star groupings lead to Pascal's death? This surely cannot be the case. Did Pascal bring about the star groupings? This would be a ridiculous idea as the planets follow their courses according to very specific laws.

Faced with this enigma, we can nevertheless see that there is a correspondence between what is expressed in a person's biography and the star constellation at their moment of death.

What has been described with the life of Pascal can be found in many other cases.

Michelangelo

The relationship between Michelangelo's life and the stars at the moment of his spiritual birth will now be described briefly. At the moment of his death the planets formed three groups in the sky. Saturn and Jupiter were rising in Cancer. Venus, Mercury and the Sun were setting in Aquarius and Pisces. The Moon and Mars were high in the sky in Taurus. So, Saturn and Jupiter were in the constellation of Cancer which in traditional astrology suggests a connection to working with matter. Dealing with matter was the central impulse in Michelangelo's incarnation.

When previously was Saturn at the position where it stood at Michelangelo's death? Saturn was in this position in 1504/05. It was the fateful year when as a thirty-year-old, Michelangelo received the task which was to determine his entire future life. He was in Florence from 1501 to 1505 where he completed his *David*. But in spring 1505 he was summoned to Rome by Pope Julius II and charged with building his tomb, a task which lasted decades.

In 1524/25 Saturn was in the position occupied by Venus, Mercury and the Sun at Michelangelo's death. This was the time

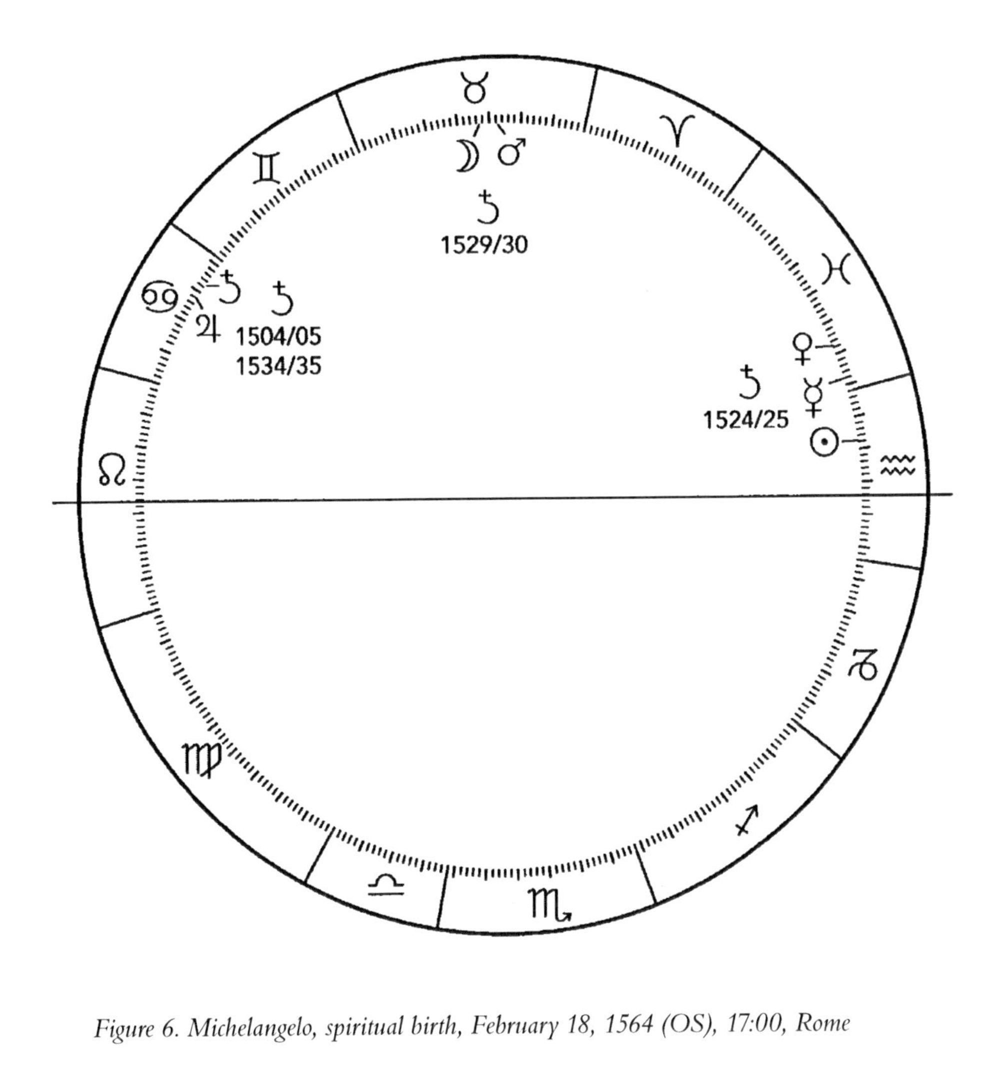

Figure 6. Michelangelo, spiritual birth, February 18, 1564 (OS), 17:00, Rome

of the disputes with those around him. Problems with his patrons intensified, the heirs of Julius II became impatient because work on Julius' tomb was not proceeding well. They demanded repayment of the honorarium which Michelangelo had already received. The disputes dragged on for years.

In 1529/30 Saturn reached the point occupied by Mars and the Moon in Taurus in the death horoscope. High in the sky they testified to the years which are amongst the most exciting in

Michelangelo's personal life. War was raging in Italy at the time, and Pope Clement VII attempted to conquer Florence. As Saturn approached the position of Mars, the imperial army advanced on Florence. Michelangelo was the architect for the fortifications and a leading member of the defence council of the city. He realized that his task was hopeless because there were many traitors within the walls of Florence who wished to turn the city over to the enemy. After warning of this to no avail he left the city but was persuaded to return. He came back to Florence but the city fell in August 1530. Michelangelo had to hide in order to avoid execution and only when the Pope guaranteed him life and freedom did he reappear in public.

Saturn was once more in Cancer in 1534/35. Michelangelo was summoned to Rome by the Pope for the second time and given the task of painting the *Last Judgment* in the Sistine Chapel. He was also appointed as the Vatican's chief architect, sculptor and painter.

Conclusion

The fact that, at the moment of death, the human being's life tableau, the fruit of his life on earth is in harmony with the cosmic constellation of that moment is evidence that man is by nature a celestial being. Pascal's death occurred at the moment when there was a correspondence between the picture in the heavens and his tableau of memories. This profound connection between the human being and the world of the stars is naturally not brought about consciously by the human being, nor is it determined by the world of the stars. Other higher powers are at work here. They work in accordance with the will of the higher self, the human being's destiny.

As already mentioned, the life tableau gradually expands until it dissolves in the spiritual cosmos. The human being's life substance returns to the world of its origin, into the cosmos from which the life body was condensed before birth. The spiritual cosmos receives the life substance which is the fruit of the life which has just come to an end.

At the moment when a human being dies, the cosmos is in a state of anticipation. What a person brings with him from his life on earth is of importance to the cosmos. This is what he has gained from his struggle with his earthly life and with the circumstances of his destiny. It is moral substance which has the greatest possible importance for the cosmos. This will be discussed further.

19. The Regions of the Zodiac

The traditional names for the constellations of the zodiac will be used here: Aries, Taurus, Gemini, Cancer, Leo, Virgo, Libra, Scorpio, Sagittarius, Capricorn, Aquarius and Pisces. These names express a pictorial language of a qualitative kind. The pictures arose in earlier times when clairvoyant faculties still existed which enabled access to the realities of the spiritual cosmos. The spiritual experiences which occurred when contemplating the sky were expressed as far as possible in a pictorial symbolic language.

Due to the disappearance of the old clairvoyant faculties we no longer have experiences of this kind. The traditional names for the constellations can therefore appear arbitrary to us.

Sometimes the same constellation was named differently by different peoples. It may well be that this difference stemmed from the differing spiritual experiences of the people in question. However, it can also be linked to the fact that different peoples expressed the *same* spiritual experience in different ways in a symbolic language.

In order to take account of the diversity of the spiritual experiences, the symbols had to have an all-embracing character. For the constellation of Aries we can imagine on the one hand the quality of 'drive,' and on the other, the selfless devotion, the defencelessness of the lamb. The traditional characteristics of Aries contain both: the battering ram and the sacrificial lamb. The traditional symbolism expresses apparently contradictory qualities: placing oneself totally at the service of an idea or impulse and bringing an idea or impulse into the world. Aries is the first sign of the zodiac and its traditional symbolism is linked to the birth of life and light in the world.

As mentioned earlier, different peoples and different cultures sometimes used different images. In Buddhism, this constellation was represented by the picture of a blind woman with a shining lamp. This also contains the same quality as that of the ram or lamb: carrying light into the world and defencelessness.

We are no longer able to experience these qualities when we contemplate the skies. We have become alienated from the spiritual realities. But they can be experienced in the spiritual world, in that spiritual realm where human souls live between death and a new birth, in the spiritual cosmos. After the ability to find a conscious way into this realm had disappeared, the pictorial language was handed down faithfully for thousands of years. We still possess this fascinating tradition. In our century, however, thanks to anthroposophy, a new living approach to the images of the zodiac can be found.

The contribution of anthroposophy

Rudolf Steiner's *Esoteric Science* describes how the macrocosm and microcosm have developed in relation to one another other over the course of a long process of evolution. Anthroposophy distinguishes three evolutionary stages in this process which have preceded our current fourth stage of the earth's development. As Rudolf Steiner explains, these three stages of evolution can be called Old Saturn, Old Sun and Old Moon. Each of these three phases of evolution takes place in seven stages under the guidance of the creative beings of the spiritual hierarchies. *Esoteric Science* describes in detail the activity of these beings in each of the above-mentioned stages.

Following on from this anthroposophical basis, in his book, *Cosmic Christianity,* Willi Sucher described how the pictures of the zodiac can be seen in connection with the sequence of the 3 times 7 stages and the deeds of the hierarchies in each of these stages. Through this approach to the process of cosmic evolution and the deeds carried out by the hierarchical beings, anthroposophy describes which spiritual realities lie behind the qualities of the traditional zodiac constellations. These qualities become comprehensible and lose their obscure dogmatic character. It becomes possible to make a connection to these qualities through thinking.

The contribution which anthroposophy can make to a renewal of star wisdom can be illustrated by means of an outline of cosmic evolution at the beginning of Old Saturn.

An outline of evolution at the beginning of Old Saturn

In *Esoteric Science* Rudolf Steiner describes the evolution of Old Saturn in the following manner. In the middle of this first stage of evolution 'spiritual perception can discern a state consisting primarily of warmth. No gaseous, liquid, or solid elements are to be found.' This is different when spiritual perception turns to the *beginning* of the Saturn period.

> What can be observed at this point has not yet acquired the character of heat that it will later possess. In trying to characterize it, we can only speak of a quality that can be compared to human willing. It is will and only will, through and through. At this point, therefore, we are dealing with a state that is all soul. If we trace this element of will back to its source, we find that it originally emanated from certain exalted beings. Through stages we can only guess at, these beings had brought their evolution to the point where, at the beginning of the Saturn phase, they could pour forth will out of their own essence.[1]

Evolution starts with a sacrifice, a sacrifice made by the hierarchy of the Spirits of Will. These are called Thrones in Christianity.

After 'will' has been poured forth for a time, spiritual beings who live in the surroundings begin to join their activity to the 'will.' The first beings which begin their work are the Spirits of Wisdom (the Christian Kyriotetes). As their name suggests, they are the bearers of wisdom, but this wisdom is also a life force. They spread their influence by radiating the light of wisdom into the dark substance of Old Saturn. The Spirits of Wisdom introduce light, life-supporting light.

> Thus this will, previously wholly without attributes, gradually acquired the ability to reflect life back into celestial space ...
>
> After a certain stage in Saturn's evolution had been reached through this interaction between will and life, other beings present in Saturn's surroundings became active. They can be called Spirits of Motion, the Christian Dynameis or Virtues.

The Spirits of Motion radiate soul activity into Old Saturn, permeating it with movement and feeling.

> As a result, it seemed as if feelings, manifestations of sensation, and other soul forces were being hurled outward from Saturn into celestial space. Saturn as a totality appeared to be an ensouled being demonstrating sympathies and antipathies. However, these manifestations were certainly not its own; it was only flinging back soul activities belonging to the Spirits of Motion.
>
> After this had been going on for some time, still other beings, which can be called Spirits of Form [Exousiai], became active.[2]

These beings have the capacity for individualization. They carry the impulse for individualization throughout evolution. In a much later phase of evolution they will endow human beings with an ego. But now at the beginning of creation they bring about a kind of 'primeval cell division': one becomes two.

> It could be said that the Spirits of Motion [Dynameis] allowed Saturn as a whole to appear as an ensouled being, while the Spirits of Form [Exousiai] divided this life into individual beings, so that Saturn then appeared as a conglomerate of soul beings.[3]

This outline of evolution at the beginning of Old Saturn must suffice for now. The intention is only to show how anthroposophy provides access to the spiritual source and background of the symbols of the zodiac. The summary given above can be of help here although it obviously cannot replace study of *Esoteric Science*. The pictures of evolution which are described there as the fruit of anthroposophical research are at first strange and surprising, but it is possible to live with them and make them your own.

The spiritual background of the zodiac constellations

In his book, *Isis Sophia,* Willi Sucher shows how we find all the 3 times 7 stages of Old Saturn, Old Sun and Old Moon spiritually inscribed in the constellations of the zodiac. The sacrifice made by the Spirits of Will (Thrones) is found in the constellation of Pisces.

> We should, however, not imagine that a gigantic process of this kind is fixed solely in the cosmic memory of the Fishes [Pisces]. We are speaking here of rounds of evolution, immeasurably long intervals of time ... These cycles or rounds of time we ought to imagine as comprising the totality of the zodiac. The inner development of the Thrones is expressed as a movement through all the constellations starting from the Fishes and going through Waterman, etc.[4]

The quality of sacrifice, the self-sacrifice and devotion which is linked to the constellation of Pisces in traditional astrology, is explained by the fact that the sacrifice of the Spirits of Will is inscribed there. In the further course of evolution — during Old Saturn, Old Sun, Old Moon and the Earth — the quality of the constellation of Pisces was developed further through the deeds of spiritual beings to what it is today.

In the next stage of Old Saturn the Spirits of Wisdom (Kyriotetes) let their wisdom-filled light radiate into the dark will substance. This stage of development is found spiritually inscribed in Aries. This characteristic of Aries of radiating light into the world is linked to this, because the influence of the Spirits of Wisdom on Old Saturn is reflected in Aries.

The next stage of Old Saturn in which the Spirits of Motion

(Dynameis) became active is spiritually inscribed in Taurus. This is the moment in evolution when the divine world set the soul of the created world in motion. As this was the stage when the divine word became active, the zodiac constellation of Taurus is still linked with the larynx and with the gift of speech. The next stage in the development of Old Saturn when the Spirits of Form (Exousiai) became active is found in the constellation of Gemini. This is the evolutionary stage when one divides into two. The characteristic belonging to Gemini of living as a duality can be seen in connection with this stage of creation.

This will suffice for the description of the deeds of hierarchical beings in connection with the evolution of the cosmos. Naturally during the developmental stages of Old Saturn there was as yet no starry sky. In place of the present-day zodiac there was a 'surrounding' of spiritual hierarchical beings who took part in evolution in turn. Each hierarchy spread its influence from a specific region of these surroundings. However, we still need to imagine that a hierarchy of this kind embraced the whole surroundings. For example, the home of the Thrones was located in that part of the spiritual surroundings of Old Saturn corresponding to the constellation of Pisces. However, from here the Thrones governed the whole surroundings. The same applied to the Kyriotetes who had their home in Aries.

This activity of the hierarchical beings continued throughout the seven stages of Old Sun, the seven stages of Old Moon and the evolution of the Earth. Nowadays we are in the fourth stage of the evolution of the Earth. The activity of the hierarchical beings during this stage is inscribed in the regions of the zodiac from where their activity arises. A detailed description of this activity can be found in Rudolf Steiner's basic books. Figure 7 on page 161 gives an overview.

It must be borne in mind when considering this overview that the seven stages of Old Saturn were described as though they had occurred one after the other. In *Esoteric Science* Rudolf Steiner points out that describing them one after the other cannot be avoided although what we call 'time' did not exist then. In

Figure 7, the evolutionary stage influenced by the Spirits of Will (Thrones) is shown as the seventh and last. In the first stage of Old Saturn the Spirits of Wisdom (Kyriotetes) let their wisdom-filled light pour in, while in the second stage the Spirits of Motion (Dynameis) are active.

Anthroposophy attempts to explain the differing qualities of the regions of the zodiac by looking at how they evolved. The zodiac only arose during the development of the Earth through a process of gradual concentration. Four developmental stages can be distinguished in this process of evolution.[5]

During the *first* stage of development, instead of the present-day zodiac there was the world of the hierarchies which exerted their influence from the surroundings. There was no star world at all, only the divine spiritual world existed: the *beings* of the higher hierarchies with which the evolving human being was closely connected.

In the *second* stage of development the divine world was no longer present as spiritual beings, but only in its *revelations*. The world of the stars then appeared. The stars were in motion and through their movement expressed the inner nature of the divine spiritual world. In this second stage the stars were therefore a revelation of the divine spiritual beings.

In the *third* stage the world of the stars is no longer the revelation of the higher hierarchies but only shows the effects of these beings. The beings themselves have withdrawn from the world of the stars. Beings of a lower order take on their tasks. They control the movements in the cosmos according to the plans of the higher star beings. These beings no longer reveal themselves, nor do they intervene. The divine spiritual no longer lives in the cosmos as revelation but only as an *effect*.

In the *fourth* stage the world of the stars becomes a created world as we know it today. Fixed laws apply: the cosmos can be calculated. It is now only the *work* of the divine spiritual. It is purely an image, deserted by the gods.

This development of the cosmos was necessary so that man could become a free being. The human being had to be released

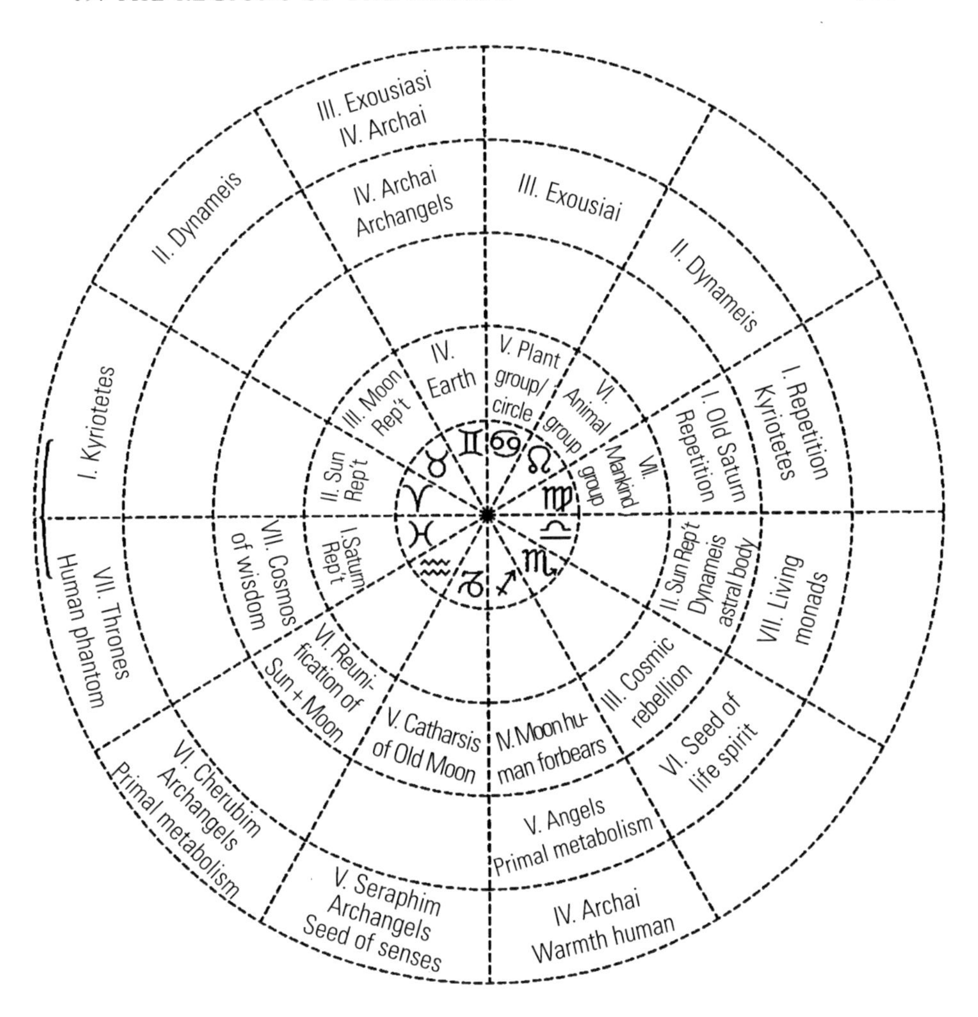

Figure 7. From: Willi O. Sucher, Man and the Stars, Cosmic Christianity, the Changing Countenance of Cosmology.

Outer circle: Old Saturn
Second circle: Old Sun
Third circle: Old Moon
Inner circle: Earth

from the spiritual realms and was placed in a world deserted by the gods.

We now live on the earth in this world of works which is only a reflection of its essential origin. When contemplating the sky nowadays it is no longer possible to feel the spiritual background of the regions of the zodiac. However, with the help of anthroposophy the emergence of the zodiac constellations can be seen and understood in connection with the realities of evolution. This enables the origins of the traditions from the past to be recognized in their true form.

20. Results of Anthroposophical Research

I will now attempt to convey the results of anthroposophy gained through study and research. A certain familiarity with anthroposophical literature must be assumed in order to understand these results properly. As well as Rudolf Steiner's *Esoteric Science, Knowledge of the Higher Worlds* and *Theosophy,* there is Willi Sucher's *Cosmic Christianity* and *Isis Sophia,* mentioned earlier. Sucher's books give an anthroposophical explanation for the different activities of the hierarchical beings that are inscribed in the different constellations of the zodiac.

It should be clear that the renewed star wisdom is based on a picture of the human being which firmly refutes the idea that man is dependent on the cosmos. Man himself creates star groupings. This can be illustrated by looking at biographies. As an example we shall look at the life of Henry Dunant, the founder of the Red Cross, first describing the dramatic events of his life and then looking at the stars at his birth into the spiritual world.

Henry Dunant

Henry Dunant, founder of the Red Cross, was born in 1828 as the son of a patrician family in Geneva. Henry's parents had decided that he should take up a career as a businessman. During his work for a Swiss trading company he became interested in a project in North Africa. Large areas there had to be cleared for planting grain. Mills had to be built in Algeria. Dunant saw good prospects for this project and founded his own company along with his partner Henry Nick. They started work although the French government had not yet approved the purchase of the land. Share capital of a million francs was issued. The necessary approvals, however, were a long time coming. Dunant therefore decided to visit the French Emperor, Napoleon III, personally to ask for his help.

Because France and Italy were involved in a war with Austria at the time, Napoleon III was in Italy. Henry Dunant therefore travelled to Lombardy. In June 1859 he arrived quite unexpectedly in an area where one of the bloodiest battles of the nineteenth century was raging, close to Solferino, south of Lake Garda.

From a military and political viewpoint the battle itself was no glorious event. The defeat of the Austrian army had actually already been decided three weeks previously in the battle of Magenta. This army had already begun to withdraw, but fighting resumed near Solferino. Forty thousand wounded, dying and dead lay on the battlefield and scarcely any help was forthcoming. In fact, there was no one there who would have been able to help. The number of wounded was so overwhelming that the few medical orderlies were completely unable to cope. At that time it was also most unusual to help enemy soldiers. Seventy percent of the soldiers died, not by being killed in battle, but through lack of care for the wounded.

When Henry Dunant saw the battlefield he broke off his journey and began to organize help. He mobilized the local population and had houses set up as field hospitals. Two churches were turned into the headquarters for the medical services. He also organized the supply of dressing materials, medicines and clothing. He forced the government to release all the captured Austrian doctors who were prepared to give assistance. The Emperor consented to this request.

After two weeks Henry Dunant left the terrible scene of suffering, completely exhausted. Word of what he had done had meantime got around, and he had become famous. But his greatest worry was for his enterprise in Algeria. He tried to obtain the necessary approvals by all means imaginable, but without success. With nothing achieved he returned to Geneva where the situation with the shareholders who were demanding interest was becoming increasingly difficult. After his return to Geneva he was also unable to forget his memories of the battle of Solferino: the images of this terrible battle were constantly before his eyes.

He began to write a book about it: *A Memoir of Solferino.* This dealt with the suffering on the battlefield, the countless wounded and dying and the inadequate aid. Looking to the future he realized that war would become more and more terrible as more and more effective weapons were invented.

He suggested the following: the founding of aid organizations for times of war which could also have a role in peacetime, for instance during floods, and natural disasters; and international agreements between states to recognize the neutrality of aid organizations.

Henry Dunant's book caught the imagination of the world in a short space of time. Positive responses and offers of help came from many countries. Dunant formed a 'committee of five' with the task of preparing to put the plans into action. This committee issued an invitation to an international conference in October 1863. During this conference, the Red Cross was founded as an aid organization. A year later a second conference took place in Geneva where an international convention of sixteen states was formed. Henry Dunant's efforts proved to be successful.

However, his company in Algeria was a disaster. The necessary approvals were not issued. The shareholders, who wanted to see interest on their capital, rebelled and started a lawsuit against Dunant. He was obliged to pay back all of the share capital. This was totally impossible for him, as it had already been used. Dunant was 39 years old when this disaster happened, and he was declared bankrupt. The city of Geneva stripped him of his citizenship and he was forced to leave. The Red Cross also expelled him and he was forbidden from linking his name with it further because this would be damaging. He was soon a discredited and forgotten man.

After being banished from Geneva he went to Paris where he lived in great poverty, sleeping outside or in a station waiting room which was open all night. Sometimes he scarcely had anything to eat, living on dry bread which people gave him. The worst was — as he said himself — that he had no money to buy new clothes. His clothes were totally threadbare. When people gave him some money he was able to rent a small room, but without any light or heating.

In 1870 the Franco-Prussian War broke out and the German army besieged the City of Paris. Despite his poverty, Dunant was active, founding an aid organization (Association de prévoyance) which collected clothes for the poor.

Dunant had been completely forgotten as the founder of the Red Cross. No one remembered him. He lived in Stuttgart for a number of years, occupying an attic room there.

When Dunant was sixty, relatives learned of his poverty-stricken situation. Thereupon they gave him an annual pension of one hundred Swiss Francs. This enabled him to afford a room and board in the Canton Hospital in Heiden not far from Lake Constance in Switzerland. He lived there for another 22 years until his death.

In Heiden Dunant's reputation was restored at the age of 67. A journalist from St Gallen, Georg Baumberger, visited him after finding out by chance that Henry Dunant was still alive. He succeeded in persuading Dunant to tell the story of his life. Baumberger was appalled when he learned of the fate and wretched situation of this great humanitarian. This must be made known everywhere! Baumberger had contacts with the press at home and abroad. Articles appeared in newspapers and magazines with the headline 'Henry Dunant is alive!' The world, which had forgotten him or assumed him dead, suddenly woke up. A Henry Dunant fund was established which collected money to improve his lot (1896). Until the day of his death Dunant had the feeling of having taken on a great debt. He suffered from the fact that he had never been able to repay his debts. He died in Heiden in the late afternoon of October 30, 1910.[1]

The life of this person, whose tragic destiny has been outlined here, is most impressive. It was really only after his death that he was viewed as the bringer of light to mankind. He set something in motion which represented the seed of a better future for mankind. Despite this, the circumstances of his life were extremely difficult and for the most part of his life he was a discredited man.

The stars

Let us look at the stars in Heiden on October 30, 1910 in the late afternoon. The two dimensional figure reproduced here must be imagined in three dimensions in the sky. The most striking feature of this constellation is the dense cluster of planets on the western horizon. The Sun, Venus, Mercury, Jupiter and Mars are within an area of 11° in the constellation of Virgo. This special concentration is in opposition to Saturn which is rising in the eastern sky. The Moon is waning and setting in the west.

On earth 'the east' is a relative concept, as what lies in the east for one person can be in the west for another. But from a spiritual viewpoint the east is a *direction.* In occult circles in earlier centuries when someone had died, this was expressed as follows: 'He has departed into the eternal east.' The reality of this pictorial language is visible in Henry Dunant's constellation. It is as though he departs into the east leaving the hard trials of fate — which he carries as a bundle or load on his back, as it were — behind him in the west. These trials of fate stand in sharp contrast to his deeper impulses which are in the realm of what is rising and emerging, represented by Saturn. The marked emphasis on the constellation of Virgo through the cluster of planets and the Moon in this constellation indicates a striving to attain a higher form of humanity. This can be understood in relation to the image of evolution in Rudolf Steiner's *Esoteric Science.* As described in Willi Sucher's books, in cosmic evolution the ennoblement or raising of the human being which started at the beginning of Old Sun and Old Moon were inscribed in the constellation of Virgo. Saturn in the constellation of Aries referred to the first stage in Old Saturn: the Spirits of Wisdom (the Kyriotetes) brought light into the dark

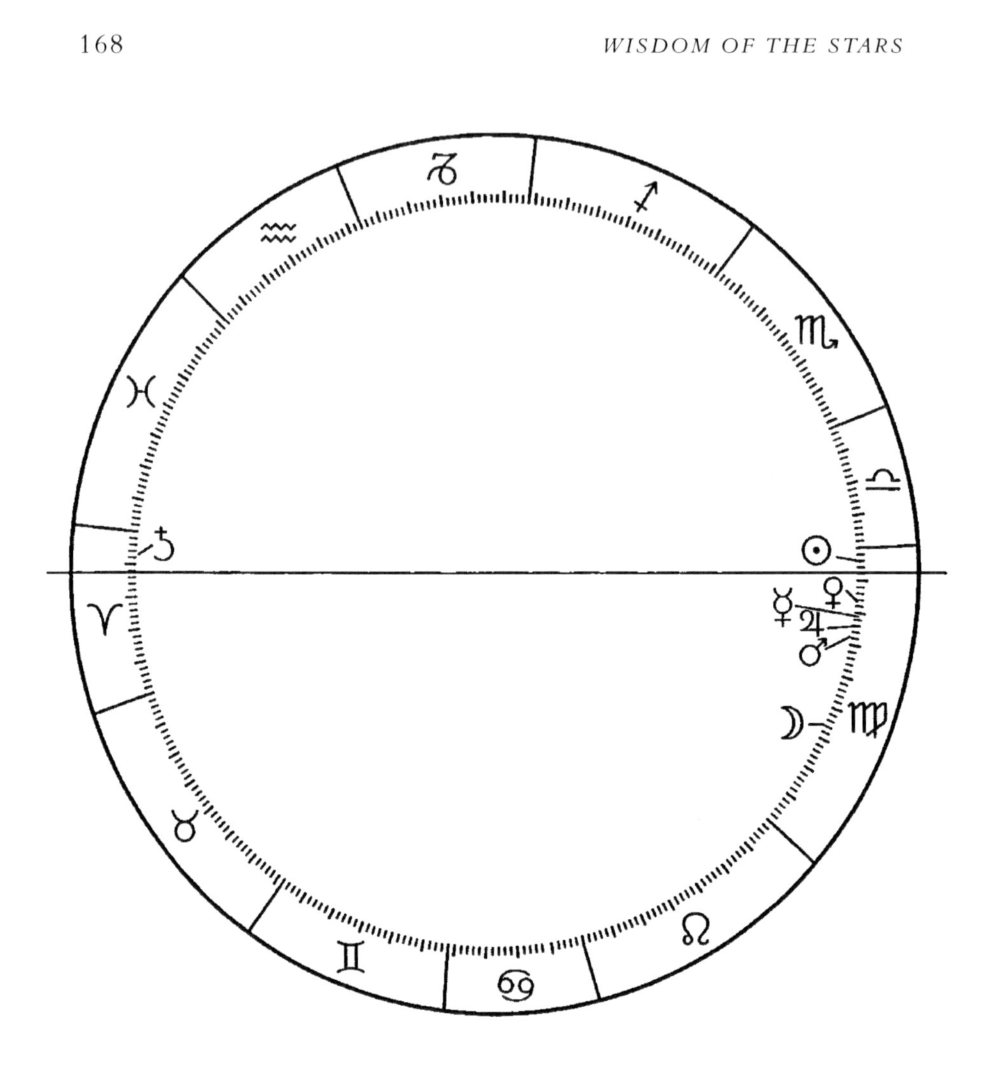

Figure 7. Henry Dunant, spiritual birth, October 30, 1910, 16:30, Heiden, Switzerland

substance of Old Saturn. Henry Dunant was a bringer of light, trying to bring light into the darkness of war.

The image of Saturn in Aries appearing through Henry Dunant indicates the oldest stage in cosmic evolution, but does not signify a return to the past. On the contrary, the person who becomes human on the earth does this as a celestial being living in the present time. He creates star groupings. In other words, he awakens ancient cosmic picture memories of creation to new life.

He gives them new form in the current times and the present-day world. The ancient images of creation are, so to speak, renewed through the activity of the human ego.

Florence Nightingale

The stars of Florence Nightingale who turned nursing into a modern profession are also remarkable in relation to this. Naturally nursing was also practised in earlier times out of a spirit of charity, but it was Florence Nightingale who gave it the status of a profession. There are many accounts of the struggle which she had to go through to achieve her calling.[2] During this she came up against great resistance from those around her.

She was best known for her action during the Crimean War of 1854–56, when she was sent by the British government to tend to the wounded and ill soldiers.

When she arrived in the barracks hospital in Scutari near Constantinople, the suffering there far exceeded her worst fears. There was a seven-kilometre-long row of beds, if the rough stretchers could indeed be called that. Thousands of wounded soldiers lay only a foot apart in long rows. The hospital wards were swarming with infectious diseases and vermin. There were neither operating tables nor medicines. The situation was indescribable. Florence Nightingale set to work in this hell. She worked day and night. She organized the work in the hospitals using systematic carefully-laid plans. Within a short time she became the hope of the ill, wounded and dying. During the day she tended to the soldiers who were undergoing operations. At night she went on her rounds in the glow of a Turkish lamp. She went from one bed to the next along the whole seven-kilometre length. She became famous as 'the Lady with the Lamp.' The soldiers kissed her shadow on their pillow when she passed by.

During her life she did many more things, such as, for example, reorganizing health care in the army. She set up nursing

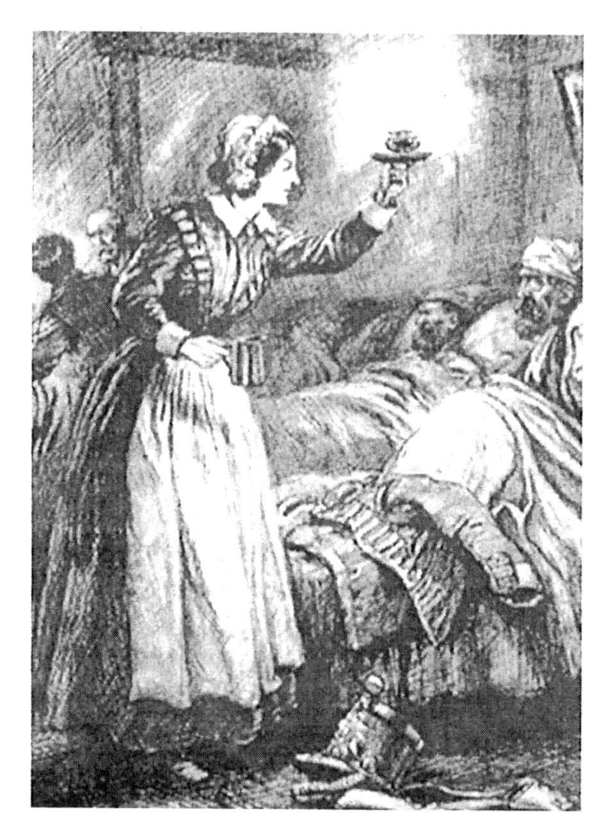

Figure 9. Florence Nightingale, the Lady with the Lamp

and midwifery training courses, and campaigned for improved health care in India.

Despite the broad range of her work she went down in history as the woman who carried light into the dark hell of Scutari with her lamp. She did not allow all the suffering around her to divert her from her task as the bearer of the light. When she was born into the spiritual world on August 13, 1910, Saturn was in Aries. Florence Nightingale became the traditional Buddhist image of the blind woman with the shining lamp. She was as though blind to the hopelessness of the situation. She carried the image of the lady with the lamp as the fruit of her life into the spiritual world.

Intermediate reflections

It should be pointed out once more that the moment of death for Henry Dunant and Florence Nightingale was neither consciously determined by them nor caused by the stars. The moment of their birth into the spiritual world was set by their higher self, their true self, completely in harmony with their individual destinies.

The renewed star wisdom looks at star groupings which people have created through their biographies and the fruits of their life on earth which they carry into the cosmos. Anyone who contemplates the relationship of the human being to the world of the stars in this manner over an extended period will be deeply impressed by the many different ways in which people bring the ancient cosmic images to a rebirth in their biographies in a totally individual manner.

What has been outlined here using the stars of Henry Dunant and Florence Nightingale is only meant as an example. From their lives on earth, other individuals could contribute something totally different at their spiritual birth with Saturn in Aries and incorporate it into the spiritual cosmos.

Dogmatic statements that 'Saturn in Aries therefore means this or that' are out of the question. For those who really live with these star constellations, the rigidly defined interpretations are replaced by far greater joy when, in the course of their research, they experience what a wealth of human substance is absorbed by the spiritual cosmos.

These remarks must be limited to providing illustrative material and a description of research which demonstrate the direction in which a renewal of the star wisdom can be found.

It will be clear from what has been discussed here that we are concentrating on what can be perceived in the sky, in other words the visible *constellations,* not the *signs* of the zodiac.

As may be known, when dividing the signs of the zodiac — which are what astrologers refer to almost exclusively — the starting point is the spring equinox. This is the point in the zodiac where the Sun stands at the spring equinox. Starting at this point, the whole zodiac is divided into twelve equal parts of 30° each. This division was introduced about 100 BC. At that time the spring equinox was in the transition between the constellations of Aries and Pisces. The first section of 30° was called Aries because it was principally the constellation of Aries which was visible behind it. The following sections were called Taurus, Gemini, Cancer, Leo, etc. after the sequence of constellations of the zodiac. However, the spring equinox moves through the zodiac constellations (about 1° in 72 years). The signs of the zodiac shift in relation to their background constellations due to this precession of the spring equinox. A shift of about 29½° has taken place since 100 BC. On account of this the *constellation* of Pisces is now visible behind the *sign* of Aries, the *constellation* of Aries behind the *sign* of Taurus etc. The points of view discussed here are based on the visible *constellations.* This does not exclude the possibility that the signs of the zodiac are also of importance for the renewed star wisdom. But experience shows that the evolutionary points of view from *Esoteric Science* explained here are related to the visible *constellations* of the sky.

21. Henry Dunant

Following on from the discussion in the previous chapter we can consider the position of Saturn at the death of Henry Dunant. This planet travels through the whole zodiac in about thirty years. It appears that Saturn was in the same position in the constellation of Aries in 1851/1852 and 1881 as it was at Dunant's moment of death on October 30, 1910. What happened in Henry Dunant's life in these years?

In 1851 he founded a Young Men's Christian Association (YMCA) in Paris. This association belonged to a revivalist movement which strove for an improvement in the spiritual and religious conditions for young people. In the years prior to this Henry Dunant had begun to be involved with the lot of the poor and sick. He visited the blind and the lame to alleviate their suffering. He also started to hold edifying lectures in prisons. He strove for social involvement and active Christianity. The founding of a YMCA in Paris was followed by one in Geneva in March 1852. Saturn was in exactly the same position in the zodiac in this month as it was at his birth in the spiritual world on October 30, 1910.

In a letter dated March 11, 1852 Henry Dunant wrote: 'Let us take up all the weapons of God by adding to piety real active and open-hearted love for our brothers in the faith; and to brotherly love compassion, that is, love to all men.' This letter shows clearly what motivated him at the time of the founding in Geneva. These foundings in 1851 and 1852 can definitely be seen as the forerunners of the founding of the Red Cross.

Unfortunately no details are known about Henry Dunant's activities in the years around 1881 — when Saturn was once more

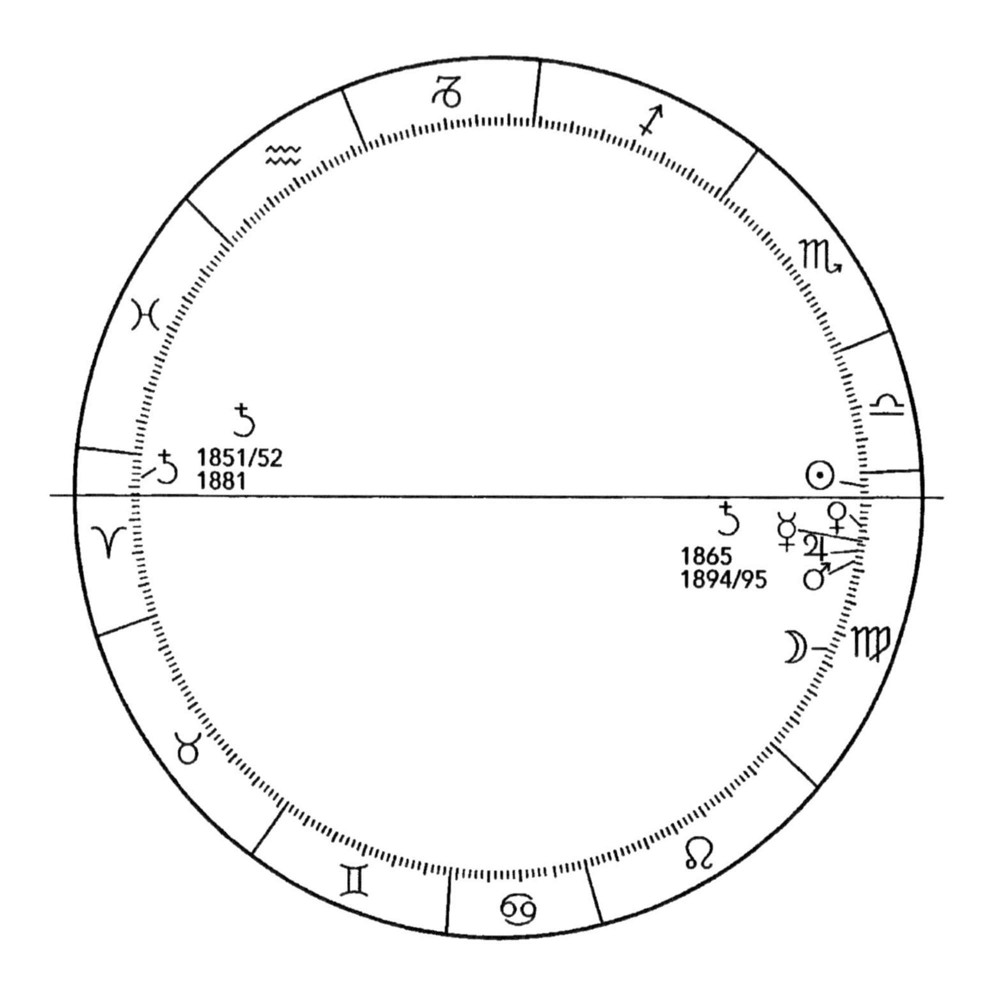

Figure 10. Henry Dunant, spiritual birth, October 30, 1910, 16:30, Heiden

in the same position in the zodiac as in 1852 and 1910. Even his place of residence is uncertain.

Let us now look at Saturn in Virgo where the other planets were located at his spiritual birth. Saturn was at that position in 1865 and 1894/95.

What took place in these years? In 1864 Henry Dunant was in Paris. He was not only beset by worries about his business in

Algeria but shortly afterwards he had to give up leadership of the Red Cross. At the Geneva Convention (August 1864) he was only allowed to play a subsidiary role, being permitted to take care of the preparation and implementation of the social events of the conference. During 1865 Dunant's business worries preoccupied him totally.

He set off for Algeria where the desired meeting with Napoleon III took place. However, the approvals which Henry Dunant required for his business were not granted. This made his situation considerably worse. The financial collapse of his company was unavoidable. He tried in vain to save his business in Algeria. Bankruptcy was inevitable and caused a breaking point in his life. The memory of these most testing ordeals was retained by the planets setting in the west in the star grouping of his spiritual birth.

On Saturn's return to Virgo in 1894/95, the thought of his rehabilitation completely occupied Dunant's life. All the documents which he had kept throughout his life were now used when writing his recollections. He was totally buried in his papers and worked day in and day out on the publication of his memoirs which he hoped would restore his reputation. An intensive inner confrontation with his destiny took place. This was further enhanced by his meeting with the journalist Georg Baumberger who asked him about his past. At Dunant's birth into the spiritual world the planets located on the western horizon recall this intensive encounter with his destiny.

Alternative approaches

What has been said so far might give the impression that the Saturn return was crucial when looking at the star constellation of the spiritual birth. This impression is not correct. This is why it should be stressed that *every* star grouping must be considered *individually*. Each grouping has very specific individual characteristics which need to be deciphered.

As an example, Henry Dunant's stars will now be considered from a different angle. At his birth into the spiritual world, the conjunction of the Sun with Jupiter, Mars, Venus and Mercury form a unique cluster. A collection like this of four planets with the sun does not occur often. This raises the question of how often a conjunction of this kind does occur? In what rhythm does it repeat? We will begin by restricting ourselves to the conjunction of Jupiter, Mars and the Sun. If the Sun was in conjunction with Mars today, when would this happen next?

The interval between two conjunctions (synodic period) of Mars and the Sun is known as the synodic period of Mars. The period shows large variations, being between 2 years 34 days and 2 years 80 days, on average 2 years and 1½ months. The exact position of the conjunction moves through the zodiac by an average of 49° during the course of Mars' synodic period. After sixteen to seventeen years it has moved through the whole zodiac so that we can say that the position of the conjunction of the Sun and Mars moves through the whole zodiac in the course of sixteen to seventeen years.

Regarding Jupiter the synodic period is about 1 year 31 days. The conjunctions of the Sun and Jupiter therefore take place every thirteen months. The position where this happens moves through the zodiac by about 30° each year. The entire zodiac is therefore traversed in the course of about twelve years.

To summarize we can say that the conjunctions of Sun and Mars move through the whole zodiac in the course of sixteen to seventeen years, and the conjunctions of Sun and Jupiter do the same in around twelve years. How often is the Sun simultaneously in conjunction with Mars and Jupiter? It is easy to see that this will happen after around 48 years ($3 \times 16 = 4 \times 12$). This is naturally a very rough calculation as the celestial phenomena show large fluctuations.

The 'predecessor' of the grouping of October 30, 1910 must therefore be sought around 1862. If we ascertain on which date around 1862 the Sun was actually in conjunction with Mars and Jupiter, we find the conjunction on August 31 and September 1,

1861. On these days the Sun, Jupiter and Mars were within 1° of each other. This very close conjunction was flanked by two further conjunctions:

— on June 25, 1859 the Sun was in conjunction with Jupiter, while Mars was 7° away;

— on October 31, 1863 the Sun and Jupiter were in conjunction while Mars was about 10° away.

Restricting ourselves to the Sun, Jupiter and Mars in the groupings at Henry Dunant's spiritual birth we can therefore find three 'predecessors' of this constellation.

What is the meaning of these constellations? What significance was attached to the time around June 25, 1859 in Henry Dunant's life? The bloodiest battle of the nineteenth century took place on June 24, 1859 at Solferino. Dunant reported this:

> Their reconnaissances, the reports of scouts, and the balloon ascents made on June 23, had given no indication of a counter-offensive or of an attack [by the Austrian army]. So, although both sides were fully expecting that a great battle would come shortly, the encounter between the Austrians and the Franco-Sardinians on Friday, June 24, was really unlooked-for ... On that memorable June 24, more than 300,000 men stood facing each other; the battle line was five leagues long, and the fighting continued for more than fifteen hours.[1]

It was exactly on this June 24 on which the battle raged from 5 am to 8 pm that Henry Dunant was approaching the battlefield of Solferino. The sight of such terrible suffering awoke the idea which some years later led to the founding of the Red Cross.

The striking relationship between the planetary constellation on 24 June 1859 (see Figure 11) and the constellation at Dunant's spiritual birth is obvious. Sun, Jupiter, Mercury and Mars occur less than 8° apart in the sky.

On August 31 and September 1, 1861 the Sun, Jupiter and Mars were again in conjunction. Nothing certain is known about Henry Dunant's life at this point.

The other similar conjunction was around October 31, 1863.

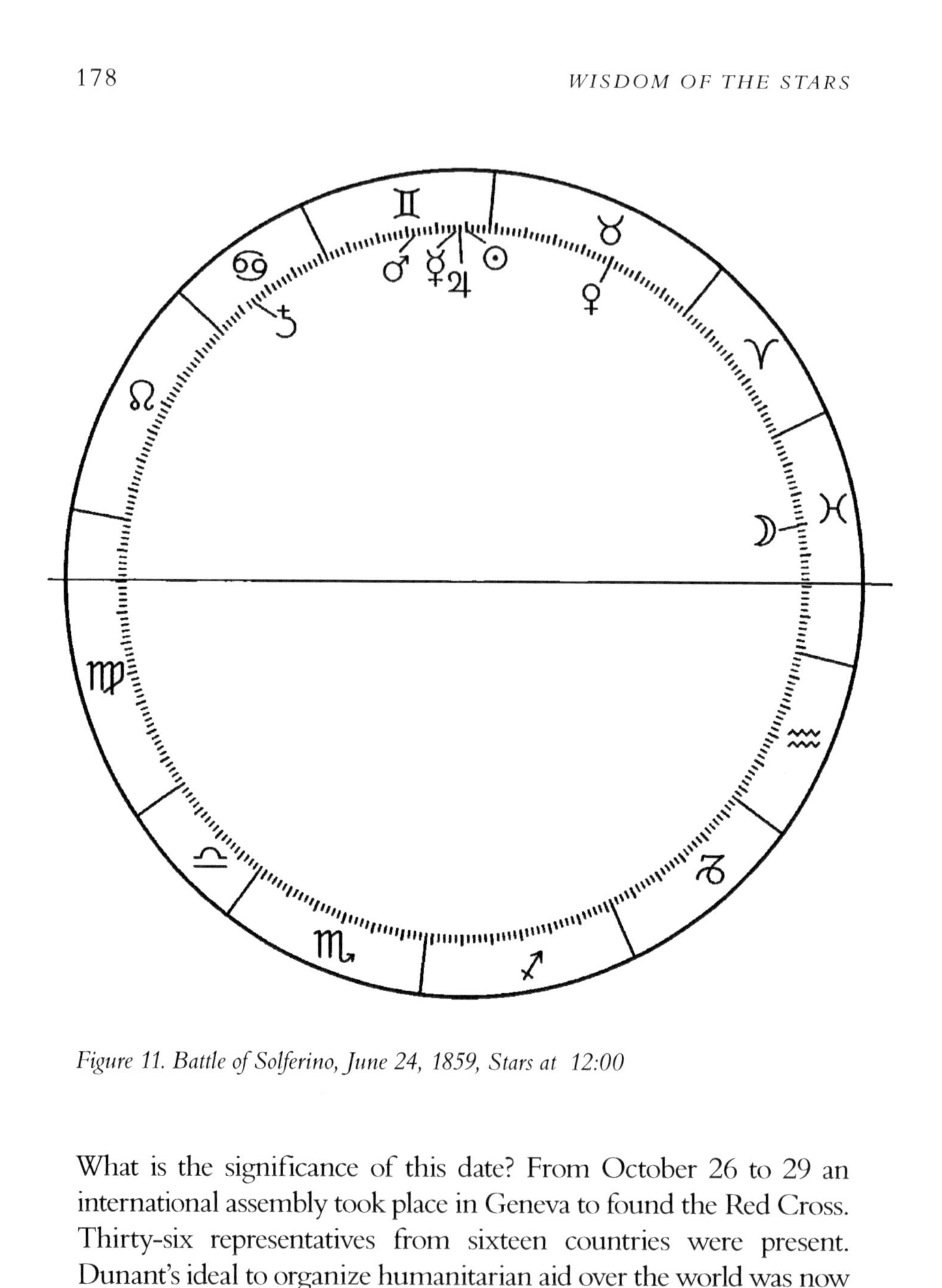

Figure 11. Battle of Solferino, June 24, 1859, Stars at 12:00

What is the significance of this date? From October 26 to 29 an international assembly took place in Geneva to found the Red Cross. Thirty-six representatives from sixteen countries were present. Dunant's ideal to organize humanitarian aid over the world was now converted into reality. The constitutional charter of the Red Cross bears the date of October 29, 1863 as its founding.

Henry Dunant's spiritual birth also shows a relationship to the stars on this day (see Figure 12). The meeting of Sun, Jupiter and

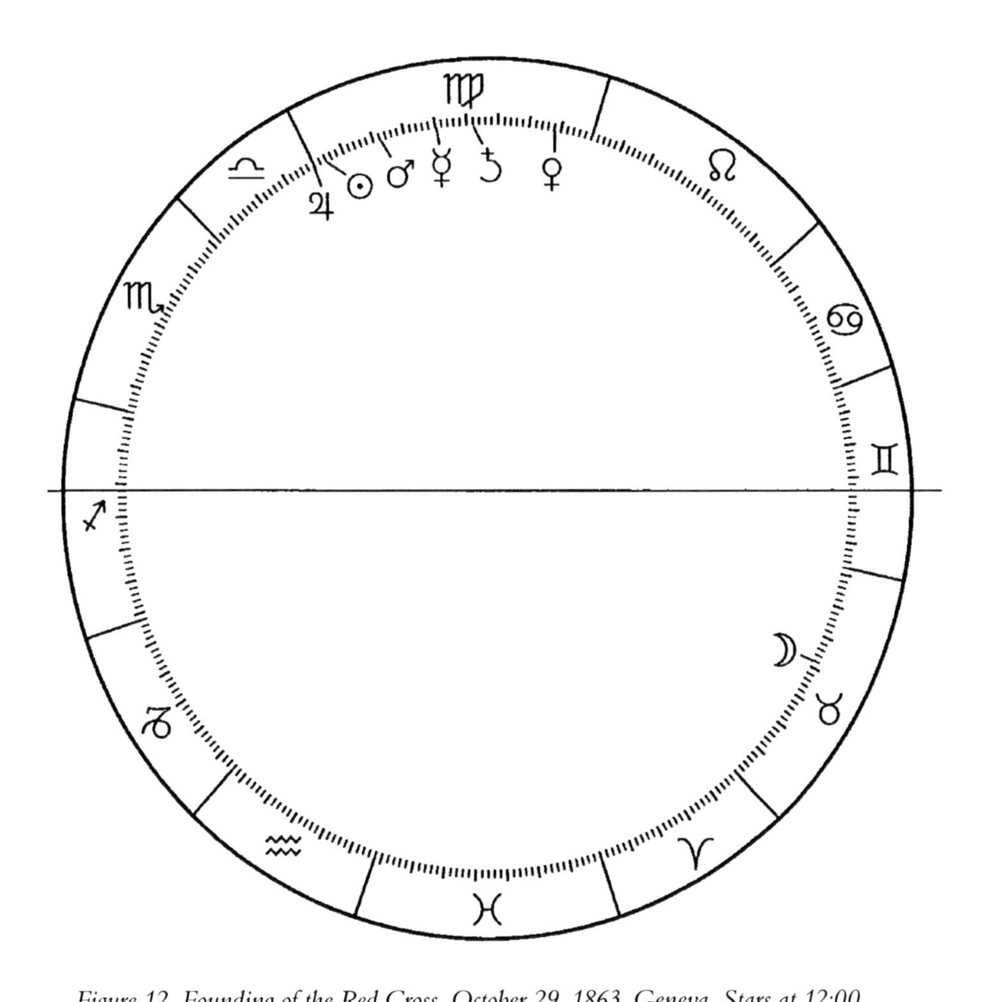

Figure 12. Founding of the Red Cross, October 29, 1863, Geneva, Stars at 12:00

Mars on October 29, 1863 took place in the same region of the zodiac as on October 30, 1910, in the constellation of Virgo which is the image of compassion. Mercury was again close by.

It is apparent that Henry Dunant's two most important initiatives, his provision of aid on the battlefield of Solferino and the founding of the Red Cross are reflected in the stars of his spiritual birth. These two initiatives were important formative moments for what Henry Dunant took into the spiritual world.

Postscript

While nothing certain is known about Dunant's life at the time of the conjunction in August/September 1861, he was probably working on his book, *A Memory of Solferino,* which was published in 1862 and within a year captured the imagination of the world. The fact that Henry Dunant had put pen to paper to write down his horrific experiences can be seen as a third important initiative by him. If he had not taken the initiative to write this book, then the founding of the Red Cross would certainly not have come about as early as 1863.

Anyone who reads the book is deeply impressed by the vivid description of his experiences. A short extract is given here:

> An old sergeant, with several service stripes on his sleeve, said to me with conviction and the utmost suddenness and cold bitterness: 'If I had been looked after sooner I might have lived, and now by evening I shall be dead!' And by evening he was dead.
>
> 'I don't want to die, I don't want to die!' shouted a Grenadier of the Guard fiercely. This man who, three days earlier, had been a picture of health and strength, was now mortally wounded. He fully realized that his hours were inexorably counted, and fought and struggled against that grim certainty. I spoke to him, and he listened. He allowed himself to be soothed, comforted and consoled, to die at last with the straightforward simplicity of a child.
>
> Some, who had gaping wounds already beginning to show infection, were almost crazed with suffering. They begged to be put out of their misery, and writhed with faces distorted in the grip of the death-struggle.[2]

The heart-rending descriptions had an enormous effect. Translated into numerous languages they roused the peoples' consciences. Henry Dunant's call evoked an overwhelming response.

Of course he did not possess any great skills for writing a book. Willy Heudtlass commented in his biography of Dunant:

'Neither before nor after did Dunant ever achieve the clarity of style and the liveliness of description that he did in this book, *A Memory of Solferino*.'[3] The incredible effect which this book had all over the world is related without doubt to the fact that the spiritual world bestowed its blessing on Henry Dunant's writing initiative. He himself described this blessing in the following way.

> When I quietly wrote *A Memory of Solferino* it was as though I was transported, governed by a higher power and filled with the spirit of God. In this state of subdued mental excitement I had an undefined feeling of inner inspiration, as though my writing were a tool for His will in order to accomplish a holy work which could be of unimagined importance for mankind in the future. Due to this presentiment I was as though compelled to write ... The power came from above, for in truth I thought nothing of myself. This book simply had to be written, I cannot express it in any other way.[4]

Anyone studying Henry Dunant's life in the light of star wisdom comes to the conviction — or at least to serious speculation — that the three star groupings of 1859, 1861 and 1863 are related to his three initiatives. The star constellation of his spiritual birth shows these three initiatives as important formative moments for what he carried into the spiritual world. These three initiatives were to provide aid on the battlefield in Solferino; to write his experiences in the book, *A Memory of Solferino;* and to found the Red Cross.

22. Saturn in Taurus

In Chapter 20 mention was made of the aspect of Saturn in the constellation of Aries. Naturally this aspect covers far more than was discussed in relation to Henry Dunant and Florence Nightingale. The way in which people can give meaning to such an aspect or star grouping at the moment of spiritual birth is extraordinarily broad and complex. To illustrate this diversity of possibilities, we shall look at the aspect of Saturn in the constellation of Taurus as an example.

We have already spoken of the sign of Taurus in relation to the second stage of Old Saturn. 'Saturn as a totality appeared to be an ensouled being demonstrating sympathies and antipathies. However, these manifestations of soul were certainly not its own; it was only flinging back soul activities belonging to the Spirits of Motion [Dynameis].'[1] In this phase the divine word became active. It brought the world which had been created in the previous phase into motion. Because the region of Taurus in the cosmos is the region of the primeval word powers which brought creation into motion, in traditional astrology this sign was connected to the larynx and to the word powers.

In order to gain a better understanding of these word powers which move the world we will look at eurythmy. Rudolf Steiner inaugurated this new art of movement as visible speech. It is based on the fact that the way in which we utter words is the same as the way in which man was spoken out of the universe. In his form and structure the human being himself is a spoken word. Rudolf Steiner described this in more detail in a course of lectures on eurythmy:

> We ask the divine spiritual powers which have existed
> from the beginning: How then did you create man in

> a similar way as the spoken word is created when we speak? How did you create man? What really took place when you created man? And if we were to receive an answer to our question from out of universal space, it would be some such answer as this: All around us there is movement, form, constantly changing and of infinite variety: such a form [*a* was here shown in eurythmy], such a form [*e* was shown], such a form [*i* was shown] — all possibilities of form in movement proceed from out of the universe, every possibility of movement that we out of the nature of our being are able to conceive and to bring into connection with the human organization.
>
> ... One can indeed say that these possibilities of movement are those which, becoming fixed, give man his physical form as it is when he reaches full maturity. What then would the gods do if they really wished to form man out of a lump of earth? The gods would make movements, and as a result of these movements capable of giving form to the dust of the earth, the human form would eventually arise.
>
> ... This is what really lies behind eurythmy. The human being as we see him in a completed form. But the form has been created out of movement ... In eurythmy we are really going back to primordial movement.[2]

These words point to the source from which eurythmy originates, the activity of the Spirits of Motion or Movement (Dynameis) in the creative word. This activity was inscribed in the sign of Taurus, as mentioned previously. Eurythmy began in 1912 and whoever considers the connections between man and the world of the stars will not see it as coincidence that Saturn was in the sign of Taurus when the art of movement of eurythmy appeared on the earth. It can be said that Rudolf Steiner answered the call of Saturn in Taurus when he brought eurythmy down from the cosmic realm of the Spirits of Motion.

An exceptional figure stood at the beginnings of eurythmy: Lory Smits (Lory Maier-Smits after 1917), the first eurythmist.

Her father died in November 1911 when she was 18 years and 7 months old. This moment of destiny had a decisive effect on her future. She had to find a profession. When Rudolf Steiner learned from her mother that Lory wished to study rhythmical gymnastics or dance he accepted her as his first pupil of the new art of movement. In January 1912 she was given the initial instruction by her mother. The first course of lessons for the new eurythmy which Rudolf Steiner held in Bottmingen near Basel from September 16 to 24, 1912 with Lory as the only pupil was crucial. In order to be able to bring down something from the spiritual world, Rudolf Steiner always needed actual questions and real situations. 'And so the very first, but only the first principles and forms of eurythmy, grew from the instruction of this young lady,' he said later, describing the development of eurythmy.[3]

On the last day of the course Rudolf Steiner said that the new art must have a name. Without hesitating for a moment, Marie von Sivers called out: 'eurythmy!.' This suggestion was immediately agreed upon. Eurythmy was born and given its name. Lory Maier-Smits was the person who enabled Rudolf Steiner to bring down the new art of movement from the spiritual realm onto the earth. She made such a strong connection to the original impulses for eurythmy that she was still able to pass these on to the younger generation in the last decade of her life in a completely pure, fresh and lively manner. It was said of her that she was always able to let the younger eurythmists have a new experience of the working of the spiritual and emotional into the visible movement.

When she died on September 19, 1971, Saturn was again in Taurus. Exactly 59 years had passed since the first training course from September 16 to 24, 1912 in Bottmingen where eurythmy came to birth through her. Saturn had passed through the zodiac twice since then and had again arrived exactly at the same position as in 1912. Saturn's position in the constellation of Lory's spiritual birth retained the memory of eurythmy's hour of birth. This showed how she had joined her destiny to this impulse.

A whole wealth of possibilities

As the zodiac represents the whole cosmos and consists of only twelve constellations, then each of these constellations must encompass a wide spectrum. What human beings can carry into the spiritual world while Saturn is in Taurus covers a huge wealth of possibilities. We can only wonder at the many different ways in which human beings can make a contribution to the spiritual world. Each constellation has to be viewed individually; due to mankind's emancipation in our time the application of star wisdom has become very individual. Only by considering many different contributions to the cosmos can a comprehensive picture gradually be built up. The development of a renewed star wisdom must of necessity begin with the consideration of parts. Anyone who attempts to gain a picture of the second stage of Old Saturn, of the effects of the Spirits of Motion (Dynameis), can imagine that Saturn in Taurus can also refer to the kind of experiences which give rise to the question: what sets the soul in motion? What do I permit to set my soul in motion? Only the highest should be permitted to move the soul.

When we immerse ourselves in the quality of this experience, in this feeling of life, then it can remind us of the famous words, 'All is vanity' (Eccles.1:2).

The famous work by Thomas à Kempis, *The Imitation of Christ,* begins with this theme. Little is known of the outer life of Thomas à Kempis. He was born around 1380 in Kempen in the Lower Rhine. Later he joined the community of the Brethren of the Common Life founded by Geert Groote. He lived in the monastery of Mount St Agnes near Zwolle in the Netherlands. There he wrote *De imitatio Christi* for his fellow brothers, a book which spread quickly and within a short time became the most widely read book after the Bible. It was translated into almost all the languages of the world.

What is the secret of this book? The work comprises four volumes. The first describes the countless wishes and desires which move the soul in unhelpful ways. 'All is vanity.' How does the human being find the way to the supreme mover? This is the way of the followers of Christ. *De imitatio Christi* is a book of exercises, a schooling which indicates the way to the supreme mover.

When Thomas à Kempis died (at the end of July or beginning of August 1471) he carried this impulse of the search for the supreme mover into the spiritual world. Saturn was then in Taurus.

Spinoza

Those who have studied philosophy will also think of Baruch de Spinoza in connection with the subject 'All is vanity.' His work was based on his own experience that what is most sought after in everyday life is fundamentally vain and trivial.

> After experience had taught me that all the things which regularly occur in ordinary life are empty and futile, and I saw that all the things which were the cause or object of my fear had nothing of good or bad in themselves, except insofar as [my] mind was moved by them, I resolved at last to try to find out whether there was anything which would be the true good.[4]

This is how Spinoza expressed it in his treatise, *On the Improvement of the Understanding* (1661/62).

Baruch de Spinoza was born and lived in Amsterdam. He was destined to become a rabbi, but because of his remarks he was banned from the synagogue (1656) and four years later also from the city of Amsterdam.

He learned how to grind lenses and this earned him his daily bread. On account of the unhealthy profession of lens grinder he only lived to the age of 44. From the age of 24 to 44 he wrote his life's philosophy: *The Ethics.* The core of his search was the question: what is it that moves the soul?

Spinoza had a deep knowledge of the human soul. He is rightly considered as the forerunner of the later science of psychology. He researched everything which moves the soul with great thoroughness — love, hate, hope, fear, despair, joy, sadness, remorse, and so on.

He approached this primarily from an everyday human viewpoint. Everything which arouses joy in our feelings and satisfies our longings is good. Everything that causes sadness and stands in the way of the fulfilment of our longings he considered bad. Each judgment over good and evil is thus determined by the kind of movement in the soul. Although man knows what is good, he can still do evil because he is moved by a force which is stronger than his reason. According to Spinoza, this all takes place from natural necessity. In his *Ethics* in particular, he provided wonderful descriptions of human emotions, driving forces and faults.

Only after he had researched the countless causes of human weakness did the moment arise when Spinoza referred to the power of the spirit. Naturally the human being needs longings as driving forces for living: man cannot exist without emotions. But these longings and passions must be regulated and guided by something higher.

Spinoza's *Ethics* is a search for the 'supreme mover,' who keeps man on the right path. The book is intentionally like a mathematics book, written with axioms, proofs and conclusions. These form a path in order to find that which has power over all vain impulses of the soul. The path which leads there is hard to find, but it can be found with effort, according to Spinoza.

He worked on a very precise and careful formulation of his *Ethics* — crossing out every unnecessary word — up to the time of his death. When he carried the impulse of his life into the spiritual world on February 21, 1677, Saturn was in Taurus, the region of the zodiac which is home to the Spirits of Motion (Dynameis).

Angelus Silesius

When Saturn is in Taurus, some may think of the familiar saying:

The Sun gives movement unto all,
And makes the Stars dance in the sky:
If I still stand immovable
No part in the great Whole have I.[5]

The writer of this little saying was the poet and mystic Johann Scheffer, who had his work published under the pseudonym of Angelus Silesius (1624–77).

As his name indicates, he was born in Silesia. He studied medicine and became private physician to the Duke of Wurttemberg-Oels. After a long preparation he renounced the Lutheran faith and in 1653 joined the Catholic Church. After his conversion he resigned from his profession as a physician and was ordained in 1661.

His important work appeared in 1657 and brought him great fame. Angelus Silesius' mystic view was that only he who felt his deeds to be carried out by the hand of God saw these deeds in a true light. God is the real mover of the human soul:

God cannot ever hide Himself — if hid he seem,
'Tis thou that hast devised a hiding place for Him.

The human being should constantly strive to follow the divine mover:

Heaven is within thee. Stay! Why runn'st thou here and there?
Thou seekest God in vain seekest thou Him everywhere.

Our deeds on earth are needed for the divine to find its purpose.

O Mystery! God's lost Himself, and therefore He,
To find Himself again, would be a new-born in Me.[6]

Two years before his death his work, originally entitled *Geistreiche Sinn- und Schlussreime* appeared under the title, *Der cherubinische Wanderer (The Cherubic Wanderer).* Or it could be said:

the angelic pilgrim who is on the way to the supreme mover. Because he who stands immoveable has no part in the whole.

When Angelus Silesius died on July 9, 1677 (Gregorian calendar), Saturn was in the constellation of Taurus.

Jacques Lusseyran

Saturn was also in Taurus when Jacques Lusseyran was born into the spiritual world. His earthly destiny had been hard, because he became blind in both eyes at the age of seven-and-a-half. But this blindness brought him a new way of seeing the world. He discovered that new organs of perception could develop in his soul. However, this perceptive ability was dependent on what was taking place in his soul. The new kind of seeing required quiet and attentiveness.

> When I was sad, when I was afraid, all shades became dark and all forms indistinct. When I was joyous and attentive, all pictures became light. Anger, remorse, plunged everything into darkness. A magnanimous resolution, a courageous decision, radiated a beam of light. By and by I learned to understand that love meant seeing and that hate was night.[7]

In this way he learned that morality (not social morality, but spiritual morality) is not just the sum of abstract rules, but an ordained order, an order of facts like an economy with light. Lusseyran's destiny forced him to observe exactly what his soul set in motion. His ability to see was completely dependent on the movements within his soul.

Jacques Lusseyran attended school along with his seeing friends. During the Second World War the seventeen-year-old founded a student resistance group. In the years following he was active in the resistance movement in France. However, he was betrayed and taken prisoner by the Gestapo and deported to Buchenwald in January 1944. He survived this time in the concentration camp and was freed by the Americans in April 1945.

He studied literature and philosophy at the Sorbonne in Paris and then became professor of French literature and philosophy.

His autobiography *And There Was Light* appeared in 1963. Further publications followed. What was his message?

> I could no longer afford to be jealous or unfriendly, because, as soon as I was, a bandage came over my eyes, and I was bound hand and foot and cast aside. All at once a black hole opened, and I was helpless inside it. But when I was happy and serene, approached people with confidence and thought well of them, I was rewarded with light.[8]

Only when he was in control of the inner movements of his soul was he able to find his direction in life. And this applies — according to Lusseyran — to every person. 'I used a blind person as an example. I could equally well have spoken of a seeing person.'[9]

Lusseyran was killed in a car accident on July 27, 1971. The manuscript of a lecture which he had wanted to give in August was later published: *Against the Pollution of the I.* It is a moving testimony to the theme of his life.

Environmental pollution threatens the earth. 'But this earth is only the lesser half of our existence, its outwardly visible field of action, its outer space. There is another space for which we are responsible: our inner space, our *I*.' This inner realm is threatened in an alarming way nowadays by outer influences which penetrate and pollute and alienate us from our I.

> My inner space does not belong to me: that is the unpleasant discovery I am forced to make. Certainly I still come across a few personal effects here and there, but rather as one comes across a needle in a haystack. Nor does my inner space belong to these others: I have not consciously made it over to them. It belongs to no one! It is littered with things. We already have automobile cemeteries; I complain about them because they ruin the countryside. And here I am becoming a cemetery myself: of words, of exclamations, of music, of gestures

> that no one makes quite in earnest, of information and instructions, of word sequences repeated a hundredfold without anyone consciously wanting them ...
>
> And yet there can be no doubt that all these noises, and these images flashing through my head, are not my own ...

Nowadays the pollution of the I progresses far faster than that of the earth because the I has its own laws.

> The *I* has certain quite specific conditions under which it will grow. It nourishes itself exclusively on its own activity. Actions that others take in its stead, far from helping, serve only to weaken it.

The activity of the I is therefore paralysed. If we do not set to work with all our strength like a lifesaver, then the truth will soon be only what the majority think and the good will be only what the majority do.

'Our *I* is fragile because it invariably diminishes when it is not active.'[10] A powerful call resounds here to put the I in motion through activity. This is the call that Jacques Lusseyran took into the spiritual world at his spiritual birth. Saturn was in Taurus.

23. Giving to the Cosmos

Man's relationship to the stars has undergone a long evolution. Through humanity's coming of age this relationship will take on a new form. The mature human being is beginning to live increasingly out of his true self and due to this is entering a *giving* relationship with the world of the stars.

It will assist the deepening of our insight into the importance of human life for the cosmos if we consider the life of Solovyov (1853–1900). We shall first look at his biography and then the stars of his spiritual birth.

Vladimir Solovyov

Vladimir Solovyov was born in Moscow in January 1853 as the second son of a well-known history professor.[1] His home was filled with a warm natural religiousness. The whole family gathered each morning and evening along with the servants before the icons in the house. Vladimir felt connected to Christianity even in childhood.

He entered grammar school in 1864. There he learned about the western world and science in particular. He was enthralled by western European natural science. These influences made him into — as he put it himself — a 'fervid materialist.' The result was a religious crisis. This gained in intensity and reached its height when Vladimir was fifteen. He was a nihilist, having lost all faith. Christianity had become a 'foolish superstition.' In order to prove this, he invited his friends to visit him at home. He tore the icons from the wall and threw them out of the window before their eyes. He studied natural science and philosophy at the University of Moscow for four years. Only after he had gone through the disappointments of this study did the faith of his childhood reawaken in his soul in a changed form.

He finished his philosophy studies at 21 and four years later made his first public appearance with his famous *Lectures on Godmanhood.* These lectures open with the question, how can a human being be God, how can God become human? The audience included Dostoevsky and Tolstoy.

In these lectures Solovyov's thoughts revolved round the spiritual being of Sophia. Who is this mysterious figure? The praises of the 'divine Sophia' were already sung in the Old Testament (Eccles.8). Many icons were dedicated to her and she was worshipped fervently, especially in Russia. Just after the foundation of Russia in 988 the first Russian church in Kiev was dedicated to her. The cathedral of the Holy Sophia still standing in Kiev was built between 1037 and 1039.

The deep connection of the Sophia being with the Russian culture is also shown by the fact that a wooden church was dedicated to Sophia the Holy Wisdom of God in Novgorod in 989. Later (*c.* 1050) a stone church was dedicated to the holy Sophia in Novgorod. Churches were also built to her in Yaroslavl and Polozki.[2]

Although the figure of Sophia was repeatedly depicted in icons, no one knew who she really was. When a Russian boyar of the fourteenth century asked the archbishop of Novgorod about the being of Sophia he got no answer: the archbishop admitted that he did not know.[3] Nevertheless, Sophia was worshipped widely amongst the Russian people as the wisdom of God.

The question about this mysterious spiritual being had an existential significance for Solovyov: it burned within him. Solovyov sought and strove for a unification of Christianity. He suffered under the eastern and western division of the church. He believed that unification of Christianity was necessary as otherwise the spiritual being Sophia could not live on the earth. Sophia is unable to embody a fragmented church. Solovyov therefore applied all his energy to strive for a universal church. In 1888 he began to write down his ideas on unifying Christianity and published two books in French in Paris in 1888 and 1889: *The Russian Idea* and *Russia and the Universal Church*. However, Solovyov's attempts to achieve something practical towards the unification of Christianity failed.

Solovyov's last work was *A Short Story of the Anti-Christ,* a shocking tale about the decisive battle between good and evil. At the end of this tale the unification of the churches takes place. At the moment when the unification of Christianity occurs, the darkness of night is suddenly illuminated by a bright radiance and a great sign appears in the sky: a woman, clothed with the sun and with the moon under her feet and with a crown of twelve stars on her head. It is a picture from the Apocalypse of John (Ch. 12). This picture points to the 'eternal feminine' in a queenly figure, to Sophia.

The question about the being of Sophia was the central theme in Solovyov's life. In past centuries many people have wrestled time and again with the question of the being of Sophia. What was unique about Solovyov, however, was that he had spiritual experiences of the Sophia being. He described these experiences in a poem 'Three Encounters.'

1. He had the first experience as a nine-year-old during a service in a Moscow church on Ascension Day 1862. He saw the shining form of Sophia surrounded by azure blue.
2. The second experience happened to him in London while studying in the library of the British Museum. Sophia only showed her face briefly. A voice told him to go to Egypt. Solovyov left London and travelled to Egypt.
3. In Cairo he again heard a voice which said: 'I am waiting in the desert.' Thereupon he went into the desert and there saw Sophia in the fullness of her being. She revealed herself to him in the desert under a shining starry sky in all her power and beauty.

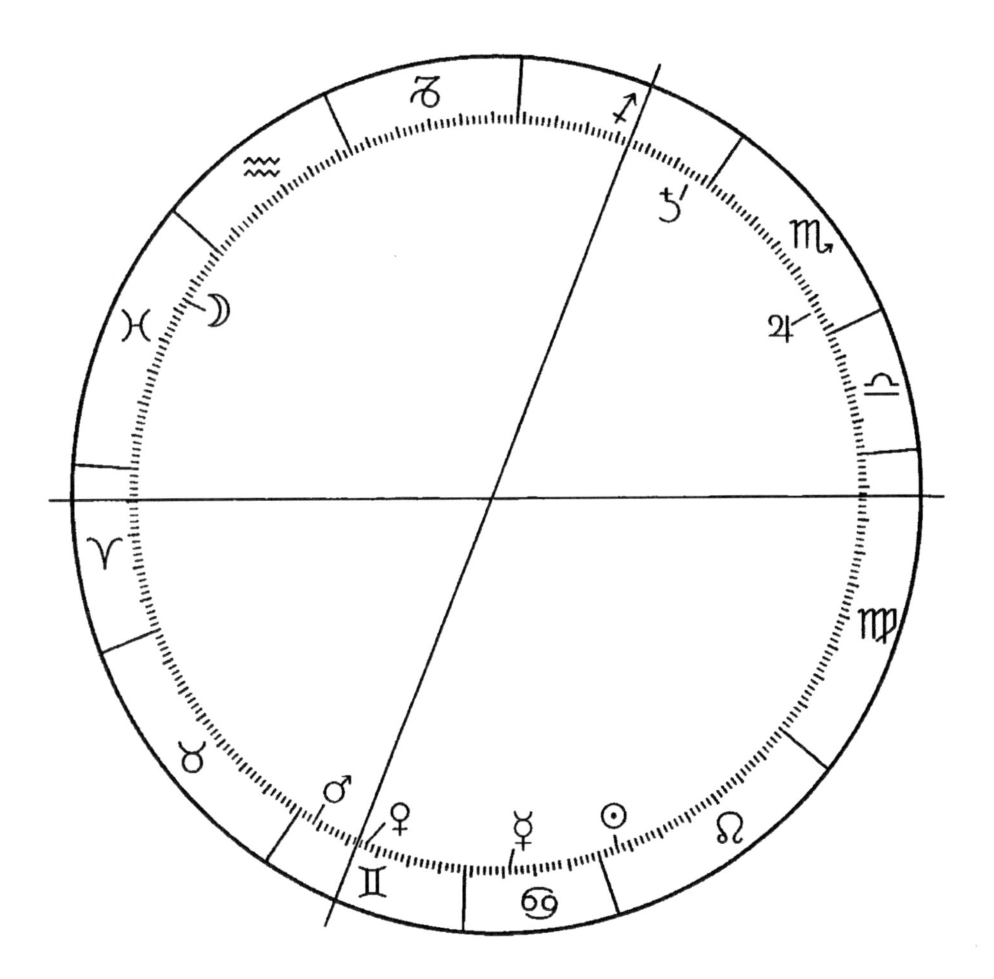

Figure 13. Vladimir Solovyov, spiritual birth, August 13, 1900 (NS), Uskoye, 21:20

These three encounters with the Sophia being were crucial for Solovyov's spiritual development. Without knowledge of these experiences of Sophia, Solovyov's life would remain incomprehensible to us. Solovyov travelled to Egypt again two years before his death. On the return journey he wrote down the three experiences for posterity.

Solovyov's life from a cosmic viewpoint

What did Solovyov take into the spiritual world as the fruit of his life on earth?

He passed through the gate of death on August 13, 1900 (Gregorian calendar) around 9:20 pm, in Uskoye near Moscow. Let us look for the stations of his life in the star writing of his spiritual birth. These stars can be viewed with the help of Saturn as the cosmic historiographer. Let us first return to his fifteenth year of life: he looked on Christianity as foolish superstition. He tore the icons from the wall and threw them out of the window. This was in 1868. Saturn was at the place in the zodiac where Jupiter stood at his spiritual birth. Solovyov's religious crisis had begun some years previously but now it reached its height. However, this crisis had a beneficial effect in his life, because the longing for the being of Sophia was born in him at this point and accompanied him throughout the rest of his life.

Saturn travelled through the whole zodiac and in 1897/98 reached the place in the zodiac for a second time where Jupiter stood at the time of his spiritual birth. Solovyov undertook his second journey to Egypt during this period, perhaps in the hopes of experiencing the divine Sophia again. In France on the return journey he wrote down his three Sophia experiences in a poem. On this journey Solovyov did not see Sophia. The fruit of this journey was the insight that mankind has a task in relation to the Sophia being and that this task can only be fulfilled by effort on the part of human beings. Jupiter (with Saturn as the historiographer) thus marked the beginning and end of the path that Solovyov followed with the Sophia being. Jupiter represents a condensation, so to speak, of his search for Sophia.

The significance of Jupiter in the star grouping of Solovyov's spiritual birth is given added emphasis by the fact that his life had a twelve-year rhythm connected to Jupiter.

1864: Solovyov entered his grammar school. He came into contact with western science and became a 'fervid materialist.' This formed the start of his religious crisis which reached its height four years later.

1876: Sophia revealed herself to him in the fullness of her being in the desert in Egypt.

1888: Attempt to unify Christianity because without this unification Sophia cannot live on the earth.

1900: Solovyov wrote his *Story of the Anti-Christ.* This described how the unification of Christianity would be brought about. When this was achieved a sublime sign appeared in the sky: the holy Sophia appeared in the image of the virgin clothed with the Sun and with the Moon under her feet and on her head a crown of twelve stars.

What is distinctive about these dates? Solovyov had made such a strong connection to the sphere of wisdom of Jupiter that he expressed Jupiter's twelve-year rhythm in his life. At each of the events mentioned above, Jupiter was in the constellation of Scorpio at that point in the zodiac where it was again located at Solovyov's spiritual birth (in 1900). Jupiter in the constellation of Scorpio thus formed an important symbol for Solovyov's birth into the spiritual world.

The importance for the cosmos

In his search for Sophia, Solovyov had created a spiritual substance which is of great importance for the cosmos. We can imagine that at his spiritual birth this spiritual substance was carried into the cosmos through Jupiter in the constellation of Scorpio. It was a new message from mankind which flowed up into the cosmos. The spiritual world received this gift from the human realm through Jupiter in the constellation of Scorpio.

This is no speculation or figment of the imagination. Confirmation can be found if similar gifts are considered which have been contributed to the cosmos by other individuals.

Consider the painter Raphael. He lived from 1483 until 1520, dying at the early age of 37. He was already famous at the age of 24 on account of his painting of the Madonna, the Virgin Mary. He painted her many times. Raphael's most famous work, the *Sistine Madonna,* was painted in 1513. The simple interpretation makes this painting the high point of all his Madonna pictures. It has never been bettered by any painter before or since.

In earlier paintings Raphael had sometimes portrayed the Virgin Mary in very realistic physical surroundings, in worldly landscapes. In contrast, the *Sistine Madonna* only touches the earth with her feet. Only the two figures right and left are a reminder of earthly reality. The figure of Mary rises above the earth, reaching up into the cosmic realm where angelic beings can just be discerned. In this painting Raphael had in reality raised the imagination of the divine Virgin into cosmic dimensions.

Tradition recounts that Raphael painted the *Sistine Madonna* in a completely different way than his other Madonnas. The other Madonnas were painted with help from his pupils. When it came to the *Sistine Madonna* he sent all his pupils away. He painted this work in complete solitude and without interruption in the course of a few weeks. He had given instructions that his pupils should leave him a frugal meal outside the door twice a day. The pupils

> saw the shining face of their teacher from a distance through the half-open door and an 'unearthly light' which filled his studio. The opinion soon spread amongst them that the Queen of the Heavens herself with her divine child had appeared to him ...[4]

It is therefore conceivable that Raphael painted the *Sistine Madonna* from a vision of Sophia.

Raphael made preliminary sketches for all his works. However, there is no trace of preliminary studies or sketches for the *Sistine Madonna,* perhaps indicating that this work was painted from a vision. This vision of Sophia gives Raphael an inner relationship to Solovyov. This relationship prompts us to look at the stars of Raphael's spiritual birth. Do they show any relationship to those of Solovyov?

Raphael

Raphael died in Rome on April 6, 1520. He had become famous because of the painting of the *Sistine Madonna.* This painting represented the 'eternal feminine' for many people at the time. In past times the eternal feminine was often portrayed standing on the moon as is the case in the Apocalypse of John. People felt that the eternal feminine was related to the moon.

Raphael died in the evening just before ten o'clock. News of his death spread quickly through the whole city. Pope Leo X broke into tears at the sad news. Many people stood on the streets, talking about the shocking news. They felt that, now Raphael was dead, Rome had changed. Rome was no longer Rome because Raphael had gone.

Those standing on the street saw that the moon had risen on the eastern horizon. This rising of the moon was seen as a significant sign from the heavens connected with the being of Raphael. People were amazed that the moon, as a symbol of the eternal feminine, rose above the horizon exactly at that moment. They realized the significance of this constellation.

It is remarkable that at the moment of Solovyov's spiritual birth the moon, as a symbol of the eternal feminine, also rose above the eastern horizon. But there is no record of anyone noticing this.

Exactly like Solovyov, at the moment of Raphael's birth into the spiritual world Jupiter was in the constellation of Scorpio and in fact at about the same position in the zodiac. The spiritual substance which was connected to the creation of the *Sistine Madonna* also flowed into the cosmos through Jupiter in Scorpio. The creation of this picture was a new message for the spiritual world from the realm of human beings. Solovyov's and Raphael's related messages both flowed into the spiritual cosmos through Jupiter in the constellation of Scorpio.

Previously we considered Solovyov's stars with the aid of Saturn. Saturn is the cosmic historian who remembers the past. We showed how, in 1868 and 1897/98, Saturn stood in the position of Jupiter in the constellation of the spiritual birth. In 1868 the young Vladimir threw the icons out of the window and this religious crisis gave birth to his search for Sophia. His fifteenth year was the key moment of his whole life. In 1898 when Saturn was again close to this position he wrote down his three experiences of Sophia for posterity. In the grouping of his spiritual birth Jupiter therefore marked the key moments in Solovyov's life, of the search for Sophia.

What do Raphael's stars show us in this respect? When was Saturn at the position in the zodiac where Jupiter stood at his spiritual birth? We are led to the period from November 1513 to August 1514 during which Saturn described a loop. Although the exact time has not been recorded, it is believed that the *Sistine Madonna* was painted at the end of 1513. This deed was received into the spiritual world in the constellation of Scorpio at the same place where the spiritual substance from Solovyov was later received. The spiritual world gathers the fruits of human lives on earth at those places in the cosmos where they belong spiritually, where they are at home. We therefore find a cosmic confirmation of the relationship between the striving of Solovyov and Raphael.

Others who sought the Sophia being could be mentioned here, for example the medieval mystic Heinrich Seuse, also known as Suso. His whole life was dedicated to the quest for Sophia, the being of eternal wisdom. He also saw the Sophia being. This was the deepest experience of his whole life about which he was barely able speak. He called the divine Sophia, whom he loved with all his heart, 'heart's bride.' After he had seen Sophia he had a picture of her painted on parchment. He placed the picture in front of him in his cell and carried it with him whenever he left the cell.[5] Heinrich Seuse was often called the servant of eternal wisdom, of Sophia. He even used this name himself. When Seuse carried the fruits of his earthly life into the spiritual world on January 25, 1366 the same sign was visible in the sky as at the spiritual births of Solovyov and Raphael: Jupiter was in the constellation of Scorpio.

These examples are intended to show that the spiritual substance which human beings attain in life are gathered by the spiritual cosmos at those places which correspond to these gifts.

24. Star Wisdom in Apocalyptic Perspective

In our times the world of the stars is viewed from a scientific standpoint. It is completely incomprehensible for this way of thinking to imagine that the deeds which human beings perform during their lives on earth could be of significance for the cosmos. A renewal of star wisdom requires a different approach than is offered by present-day astronomy. Anthroposophy views the cosmos as a living spiritual organism which requires nourishment. For this huge organism to survive it requires the spiritual nourishment which people carry into the world of the stars at their spiritual birth. According to Rudolf Steiner,

> [The human being] brings into this spiritual world what he has experienced on earth while waking and sleeping.
>
> Just consider that these experiences are the nourishment of the cosmos; that they are continuously needed by the cosmos in order to live on. Whatever we experience on earth in the course of an easy or hard life is carried by us into the cosmos after death. We thus feel how our being as man is dissolved into the cosmos to furnish its nourishment. These experiences, undergone by man between death and a new birth, are of overwhelming grandeur, of immeasurable loftiness
>
> ... What we pass through here on earth is divided and given to the cosmos: so that it might nourish the cosmos and enable it to live on; so that the cosmos might receive new incentives for the movement of its stars, the sustenance of its stars. As we must partake of physical nourishment in order to live as physical ... [human beings]

> between birth and death, so must the cosmos partake of human experiences, take them into itself.[1]

An apocalyptic perspective opens up. The Apocalypse of John describes how the present-day world will finally end. The world of the stars will also come to an end. The stars will fall down onto the earth, the sun and moon will be darkened. The world of the stars will dissolve completely. The only thing which will remain is the spiritual activity of human beings, what people have radiated into the spiritual cosmos. A *new* heaven and a *new* earth will be produced. They will be formed from what human beings have taken up into the cosmos as spiritual substance through their free deeds.

This is a dramatic future perspective! At the end of the existence of the earth something will have to have arisen which will survive when heaven and earth have passed away: a spiritual fruit created by human beings. Thanks to this fruit a new earth and a new heaven will be able to arise. The spiritual substance created by human beings will enable evolution to continue.

In *Esoteric Science* Rudolf Steiner described how the human being was created from the cosmos, from the surroundings. There are twelve cosmic regions in these surroundings. Mankind exists thanks to the spiritual beings who acted from these twelve regions. The gifts from these twelve regions formed the human being. Man, who has now become independent and responsible, has the possibility of giving back gifts to the cosmos. He is called to do this because evolution proceeds from receiving to giving. Previously the human being was a receiver. From now onwards he will increasingly become a giver to the world of the stars. The fruits of his life which the human being brings with him to the spiritual world at his spiritual birth will be gathered by the spiritual powers. As was described in Chapter 23, they will be received in the appropriate cosmic regions in order to provide substance for a future development.

We human beings therefore have a great responsibility towards the spiritual cosmos. Much is said nowadays about our responsibility for other people and other nations and about our responsibility for the environment, for the earth. However, nothing is ever said about our responsibility towards the cosmos, the world of the stars! But this responsibility is enormous. Each human being has this responsibility for the cosmos because he is a celestial being, a cosmic being. After all, he spends the larger part of his whole existence in the star world, in life between death and a new birth. The knowledge that the human being is a cosmic being was forgotten during the dark age. That era ended in 1879. The beginning of the age of light means that we have to become conscious of and take up our responsibility towards the spiritual cosmos.

A reversal in the relationship of man to the world of the stars

Nowadays a reversal is taking place in the relationship between man and the world of the stars. Let us try to describe this.

In ancient times it was the task of the mystery priests to study the will of the gods through careful observation of the movements in the stars. Study of the heavens culminated in the ability to acquire knowledge about a person's destiny from the stars at their birth. The birth aspects revealed how the gods had arranged the birth in order to achieve *their* intentions. The mystery priests said: 'If you know the heavenly circumstances at the moment when a person is born, then you know how the heavens have guided this person down onto the earth in order to achieve the aims of the gods.'

In the course of history this consciousness of the world of the stars had to fade because the gods intended to create man as a free being. This freedom appeared in the fact that it became possible for human beings to form abstract intellectual concepts, concepts which do not restrict man. This awareness of freedom was only able to arise in the evolution of mankind when the consciousness from which astrology arose had died out, a consciousness which made mankind appear as a being who carried out the will of the gods.[2]

Nowadays, in the age of the consciousness soul, humanity has started to develop its freedom. This is why the gods look differently on human beings than they did in earlier times. Now they look to see to what extent their ideal of creating a free human being has been fulfilled, to what degree the human being has become able to act in freedom. This cannot be seen at the moment of birth, but only at the moment of death, when the human being returns to the world of the stars and the gods see what human beings bring to them. Nowadays every human being has to confront his destiny in freedom to an increasing degree. When someone wrestles with the questions in life honestly and sincerely, this is important for the star world. Rudolf Steiner pointed to this fact in a verse:

> The stars spoke once to man.
> It is world-destiny that they are silent now.
> To be aware of the silence
> Can become pain for earthly man.
> But in the deepening silence there grows and ripens
> What man speaks to the stars.
> To be aware of the speaking
> Can become strength for spirit-man.[3]

Nowadays we can observe which human gifts are gathered at particular places in the cosmos. This gives us a completely new understanding of the world of the stars. Traditional astrology observed the world of the stars with the aim of learning about the human being. The new star wisdom observes the fruits of experience which human beings take into the cosmos at their spiritual birth. This star wisdom therefore follows the opposite path. The human being and his struggles in life are the starting point for looking at the cosmos, thus gaining a new knowledge of the world of the stars. This change of direction is crucial for the founding of a star wisdom which has a future perspective.

When a person is born into the spiritual world nowadays the world of the stars is filled with anticipation. The cosmos receives what is radiated upwards by human souls passing through the gate of death. Since the mystery of Golgotha the earth has become a star, radiating into the cosmos. Because all human beings now radiate the fruits of their life on earth up into the cosmos, Rudolf Steiner called the earth a 'human star.' This significance of the human being for the world must be recognized nowadays. Then, as Rudolf Steiner said, something different will be able to take the place of the old astrology.

> In our times, we have to take hold of what has been given to us: intellectualism and consciousness of freedom. If we take hold of them in the right way ... then we find the Christ forces in the depths of our soul. We will then realize that while people looked to the constellation of the stars in ancient times to understand human destiny on earth, we must now look to the human being. In this way we learn how the human being, permeated by the Christ substance here on earth while possessing full humanness, then lights up for the universe. The human being lights up as the star of humanity after having gone through the portal of death.
>
> This is the spiritual humanism that can take the place of ancient astrology.[4]

Naturally the new relationship between the human being and the star world is only beginning. This relationship will only gain in strength through the progressive individualization of the human being. New spiritual realities will be created through conscious human deeds. As a result, in the future the star groupings at spiritual birth will become increasingly meaningful, significant and eloquent. The wonderful and magnificent event of the stars of a person's birth into the spiritual world is already there. Anthroposophy enables us to see it with respect and reverence. It also makes it clear that what is remarkable and significant about this grouping of stars results from the fact that Christ died and rose again. Looking at the stars of a spiritual birth we may then truly say: 'Christ has risen, truly risen! This fact is visible in the starry sky.' We can again and again be filled with wonder that the consequences of the mystery of Golgotha appear in the starry sky. This reveals the cosmic dimension of the being of Christ. It is the cosmic Christ who says, 'heaven and earth will pass away, but my words will not pass away.' (Matt.24:35). These words speak of a Christianity which is not just to be found in books, but — as Rudolf Steiner said — of a Christianity which is also to be found in the stars.[5]

The constellations were calculated using the 'Triform Chart and Ephemeris Program' by Peter Treadgold. The exact data are (applied to zodiac signs):

	☉	☽	☿	♀	♂	♃	♄
Spiritual birth of Dunant	6° 22 ♏	9° 53 ♎	28° 12 ♎	29° 39 ♎	25° 24 ♎	27° 26 ♎	2° 50 ♉
Spiritual birth of Michelangelo	9° 8 ♓	3° 48 ♊	18° 44 ♓	24° 23 ♓	0° 33 ♊	29° 9 ♋	27° 16 ♋
Spiritual birth of Pascal	26° 5 ♌	24° 15 ♎	29° 40 ♌	15° 25 ♋	5° 21 ♎	7° 27 ♏	28° 45 ♏
Solovyov	20° 30 ♌	1° 00 ♈	4° 3 ♌	11° 12 ♋	2° 27 ♋	1° 23 ♐	28° 44 ♐
Battle of Solferino	2° 22 ♋	12° 22 ♈	3° 55 ♋	6° 58 ♊	10° 35 ♋	3° 16 ♋	10° 18 ♌
Founding of the Red Cross	5° 35 ♏	8° 35 ♊	17° 29 ♎	28° 51 ♍	26° 48 ♎	7° 18 ♏	11° 54 ♎

Notes

1. The Beginnings of a Wisdom of the Stars

1 Teichmann, *Kultur der Empfindungsseele,* Dietz, *Metamorphosen des Geistes,* Steiner, *Esoteric Science* and *Theosophy.*
2 Bock, *Genesis,* p. 102.

2. The Egyptian Star Religion

1 Steiner, *Antworten der Geisteswissenschaft,* lecture of Feb 16, 1911, p. 371.
2 Faulkner, *Ancient Egyptian Texts,* p. 19.
3 Knappich, *Geschichte der Astrologie,* p. 14.
4 Knappich, *Geschichte der Astrologie,* p. 14.
5 Assmann, *Ma'at,* p. 218.
6 This and the subsequent examples are taken from Brunner-Traut, *Gelebte Mythen*, pp. 21ff.
7 Steiner, *Antworten der Geisteswissenschaft,* page 370. Also, Ernst, *Kultur und Kunst Ägyptens.*

3. The Mesopotamian Star Religion

1 Kugler, *Sternkunde und Sterndienst in Babylon,* quoted in Pannekoek, *A History of Astronomy,* p. 33.
2 Geissler, *Astrologie, Geschichte, Entwicklung, Bedeutung,* p. 19.

4. The Dark Age

1 Knappich, *Geschichte der Astrologie*, p. 36. A large number of sky omens are in Ungnad, *Religion der Babylonier und Assyrer.*
2 Thompson, *Reports of the Magicians,* p. 274, quoted in Pannekoek, *A History of Astronomy,* p. 45.
3 Steiner, *Spiritual Guidance of the Individual and Humanity,* lecture of June 3, 1911, p. 60.
4 Fischer, *Geburt der Hochkultur in Ägypten und Mesopotamien*. Similar statements have been handed down from Egyptian culture around 1300 BC. See Teichmann, *Die ägyptischen Mysterien,* pp. 276–280.

5. The Fate of the Star Mysteries

1 Steiner, *Esoteric Science* and *Cosmic Memory.*
2 Steiner, *Esoteric Science,* Steiner, *Knowledge of the Higher Worlds.*

3 Steiner, *Mysteries of the East and of Christianity,* lecture 3 of Feb 5, 1913.
4 Bock, *Moses,* p. 21.
5 For the Sothis periods see the Steiner, *Antworten der Geisteswissenschaft,* lecture of Feb 16, 1911, and Uehli, *Kultur und Kunst Ägyptens;* von Gleich, *Marksteine der Kulturgeschichte;* and Gsänger, *Mysteriengeschichte der Menschheit.* Concerning this turning point see Steiner, *Antworten der Geisteswissenschaft,* lecture of March 9, 1911.
6 Steiner, *Antworten der Geisteswissenschaft,* lecture of March 9, 1911.

6. The Hebrew People

1 Bock, *Genesis,* p. 98.
2 Steiner, *East in the Light of the West,* lecture of Aug 30, 1909.
3 Steiner, *Gospel of St Matthew,* lecture of Sep 2, 1910.
4 Steiner, *Gospel of St Matthew,* lecture of Sep 2, 1910, and Thieben, *Rätsel des Judentums,* pp. 66f.

7. The Emergence of the Birth Horoscope

1 Sachs, Babylonian Horoscopes, *Journal of Cuneiform Studies,* 1952 Vol. 6, quoted by Knappich, *Geschichte der Astrologie.*
2 Schäfer, *Vom Sternenkult zur Astrologie,* p. 77.

8. Contrasting World Views

1 The meaning of the Greek word *stoicheia,* translated as 'spirits of the universe,' includes the stars and can refer to the twelve signs of the zodiac in particular. See Voss, *Astrologie christlich.*

9. Advisers to the Caesars in Rome

1 Knappich, *Geschichte der Astrologie,* p. 77.
2 Knappich, *Geschichte der Astrologie;* Parker, *A History of Astrology;* Schäfer, *Vom Sternenkult zur Astrologie.*
3 Cited after Schäfer, *Vom Sternenkult zur Astrologie,* p. 150.
4 Schäfer, *Vom Sternenkult zur Astrologie,* p. 156.
5 von Sementowsky-Kurillo, *Mensch griff nach den Sternen*, p. 133.

10. The Cult of Mithras, an Astrological Religion

1 The description of the cult temples is based on Schütze, *Mithras,* Chapter 'Die Kultstätte und das Altarbild;' Clauss, *Mithras,* Chapter 'Kulträume.'
2 Schütze, *Mithras,* pp. 66 ff.
3 Schütze, *Mithras,* p. 83.
4 Schütze, *Mithras,* p. 83.
5 Macrobius, *Dream of Scipio,* 1.12.13–14. Quoted from Clauss, *Mithras,* p. 21.
6 Servius, *Commentary on the Aeneid*, 6.714.
7 Schütze, *Mithras,* p. 93.
8 Schütze, *Mithras,* pp. 88/89.

9 Schütze, *Mithras,* p. 189.
10 Schütze, *Mithras,* p. 96.

11. The Views of the Christian Church

1 Eva Fleischmann-Kessler, *Funktion und Bedeutung der Himmelskörper in der 'Summa Theologica' des Thomas von Aquin,* Dissertation in the Department of Philosophy, University of Zurich (1984). The quotations which follow were taken from a summary article 'Astrologische Thesen bei Thomas von Aquin,' in the journal, *Astrolog,* 1985. Vol. 27, Aug 23.
2 The letter was translated (into German) by Eugen Kolisko, published in *Natura*, Dec 1928 / Jan 1929, Vol. 3, No. 6/7. The English quotation here is translated from that version.
3 *Summa Theologica,* I Q 115, A 4 and 3. Quoted from Voss, *Astrologie christlich.*

12. The Flowering and Decline of Astrology

1 Knappich, *Geschichte der Astrologie,* p. 264.
2 Knappich, *Geschichte der Astrologie,* p. 263.
3 Geissler, *Astrologie, Geschichte, Entwicklung, Bedeutung,* p. 121.

13. Boundaries of Knowledge

1 Hemleben, *Galileo Galilei*, pp. 154ff.
2 Emil Du Bois-Reymond, in a lecture 'Über die Grenzen des Naturerkennens' at the fifty-fourth gathering of German natural scientists and physicians in Leipzig Aug 14, 1872.
3 Steiner, *Rosicrucianism and Modern Initiation,* lecture of Jan 6, 1924.
4 Steiner, *Esoteric Science;* Steiner, *Knowledge of the Higher Worlds;* Steiner, *The Stages of Higher Knowledge.*
5 Floride, *Weg zu den Hierarchien.*
6 Steiner, *Rosicrucianism and Modern Initiation,* lecture of Jan 6, 1924.
7 For details on Agrippa's biography see Kuper, *Agrippa von Nettesheim;* Steiner, *Die Mystik im Aufgange des neuzeitlichen Geisteslebens;* Morley, *Cornelius Agrippa.*

14. Astrology in the Age of Natural Science

1 Steiner, *Menschengeschichte im Lichte der Geistesforschung,* lecture of Nov 9, 1911.
2 As was usual at the time, he had the lecture read out by a pupil, Jakob Milich. There is a translation into German by Igo Dammer in Hoppmann, *Astrologie der Reformationszeit.*
3 Hemleben, *Paracelsus,* p. 186.
4 Paracelsus, *Paragranum,* (Sudhoff 1.8.100), in *Naturwissenschaftliche und medizinische Schriften;* Daems, *Denn der Himmel ist der Mensch.*
5 Steiner, *Natur- und Geistwesen,* lecture of Nov 7, 1911, p. 20.
6 Hemleben, *Kepler.*
7 Harburger (ed.), *Johannes Keplers 'Kosmische Harmonie,'* p. 195.

8 Strauss, & Strauss-Kloebe, *Astrologie des Johannes Kepler.*
9 Voltmer, *Rhythmische Astrologie.*
10 Choisnard, *Le méthode statique et le bon sens en astrologie.*

15. Astrology and Anthroposophy

1 Bock, *The Life and Times of Rudolf Steiner,* Vol. 1, pp. 180–86.
2 Lindenberg, *Rudolf Steiner, eine Biographie,* p. 503; Hemleben, *Rudolf Steiner,* p. 78; Steiner, *Mysteries of the East and of Christianity,* lecture of Feb 3, 1913.
3 Steiner, *Human and Cosmic Thought,* p. 57.
4 Steiner, *Rosicrucianism and Modern Initiation,* lecture of Jan 6, 1924.
5 Steiner, *Rosicrucianism and Modern Initiation,* lectures of Jan 4 and Jan 11, 1924.
6 Steiner, *Mysteries of the East and of Christianity,* Lecture of Feb 6, 1913.

16. A New Relationship Between Man and the World of the Stars

1 Steiner, *Christ and the Spiritual World,* lecture of Jan 1, 1914.
2 Voss, Gerhard, *Astrologie christlich;* Von Heymann, *Wo ist der rote Faden?* Staubinger, *Du sollst keine anderen Götter neben mir haben;* Kochanek, *Horoskop als Schlüssel zum Ich;* Böhringer, *Astrologie.*
3 *Catechism of the Catholic Church,* CCC 2116.
4 Steiner, *Spiritual Guidance of the Individual and Humanity,* pp. 65f.
5 Steiner, *New Spirituality,* lecture of Oct 31, 1920.
6 Steiner, *Karma of Untruthfulness,* Vol. 2, lecture of Jan 21, 1917, p. 157.

17. Fundamentals of a Spiritual Star Wisdom

1 With regard to imagination, inspiration and intuition see Steiner, *Esoteric Science; Stages of Higher Knowledge.*
3 Steiner, *Theosophy; Esoteric Science; Life Between Death and Rebirth; Between Death and Rebirth.*

18. The Stars at a Spiritual Birth

1 Steiner, *Karma of Untruthfulness,* Vol. 2, lecture of Jan 21, 1917.
2 Béguin, *Blaise Pascal.*
3 Koch, *Michelangelo.*
4 Steiner, *Initiationswissenschaft und Sternenerkenntnis,* lecture of July 27, 1923; and *Esoterische Betrachtungen karmischer Zusammenhänge,* Vol. 5, lecture of June 10, 1924.

19. The Regions of the Zodiac

1 Steiner, *Esoteric Science,* pp. 135, 140.
2 Steiner, *Esoteric Science,* pp. 140f.
3 Steiner, *Esoteric Science,* p. 142.
4 Sucher, *Isis Sophia II,* pp. 81f.
5 Steiner, *Anthroposophical Leading Thoughts,* 'The Activity of Michael and the Future of Mankind,' Oct 25, 1924.

20. Results of Anthroposophical Research

1 F. Christ, *Henry Dunant.*
2 Woodham-Smith, *Florence Nightingale;* Brown, *Florence Nightingale.*

21. Henry Dunant

1 Dunant, Henry, *A Memory of Solferino,* p. 4.
2 Dunant, Henry, *A Memory of Solferino,* p. 14.
3 Heudtlass, *J. Henry Dunant,* p. 46.
4 Heudtlass, *J. Henry Dunant,* pp. 52f.

22. Saturn in Taurus

1 Steiner, *Esoteric Science,* p. 141.
2 Steiner, *Eurythmy as Visible Speech,* pp. 35f.
3 See the obituary for Lory Maier-Smits in *Mitteilungen aus der anthroposophischen Arbeit in Deutschland,* Vol. No. 98, Christmas 1971. On Lory Maier-Smits see also *Wirken Rudolf Steiners,* Vol. 3: 1907 to 1917, p. 26; Maier-Smits, 'Die Anfänge der Eurythmie.' In *Wir erlebten Rudolf Steiner.*
4 Nadler, Steven, *Spinoza, a Life.*
5 Silesius, *The Cherubinic Wanderer,* 339 (VI.42)
6 Silesius, *The Cherubinic Wanderer,* 33 (V.65); 122 (I.82); 170 (I.201).
7 Lusseyran, *What One Sees Without Eyes,* p. 54.
8 Lusseyran, *And There Was Light,* p. 13.
9 Lusseyran, *What One Sees Without Eyes,* p. 61.
10 Lusseyran, *What One Sees Without Eyes,* pp. 95, 101, 102, 103, 118.

23. Giving to the Cosmos

1 Waage, *Unsichtbare Kontinent.* Details on Solovyov's biography were taken from this book and also from Bayer, *Solowiew.*
2 Prokofieff, *Die geistigen Quellen Osteuropas,* p. 132.
3 Waage, *Unsichtbare Kontinent,* p. 82.
4 Prokofieff, *Ewige Individualität,* p. 324, note 94, and p. 352, note 229.
5 Lehmann (ed.), *Heinrich Seuses deutsche Schriften,* Vol. 1 p. 89.

24. Star Wisdom in Apocalyptic Perspective

1 Steiner, *Man's Being, his Destiny,* lecture of May 16, 1923, pp. 14–16.
2 Steiner, *Earthly Knowledge and Heavenly Wisdom,* lecture of Feb 10, 1923, p. 58.
3 Rudolf Steiner, *Verses and Meditations* (Verse for Marie Steiner, December 25, 1922).
4 Steiner, *Earthly Knowledge and Heavenly Wisdom,* lecture of Feb 10, 1923, p. 67.
5 Steiner, *Christus und die menschliche Seele,* lecture of July 12, 1914, p. 160.

Bibliography

Adler, Oskar, *Das Testament der Astrologie,* 4 volumes, Munich 2000.

Agrippa von Nettesheim, *Of the Vanitie and Uncertaintie of Artes and Sciences (De Incertidine et Vanitate Scientarum Atque Artium),* ed. Catherine M. Dunn, California State University Foundation 1974.

Andrea, Johann Valentin, *Die Chymische Hochzeit des Christian Rosenkreutz,* Freies Geistesleben, Stuttgart 1957.

—, *The Chemical Wedding of Christian Rosenkreutz,* Tr. Joscelyn Godwin, Phanes, USA 1994.

Assmann, Jan, *Ma'at, Gerechtigkeit und Unsterblichkeit im alten Ägypten,* Munich 1999.

Aquinas, Thomas, *see* Thomas Aquinas

Augustine, *The Confessions of St Augustine,* ed. Rex Warner, Penguin, New York 1963.

—, *The City of God,* Tr. Henry Bettenson, Penguin, UK 1972.

Bayer, C., *Solowiew,* The Hague 1964.

Béguin, Albert, *Blaise Pascal in Selbstzeugnissen und Bilddokumenten,* Rowohlt, Hamburg.

Bock, Emil, *Genesis,* Floris Books, Edinburgh 1983.

—, *The Life and Times of Rudolf Steiner,* Floris Books, Edinburgh 2008.

—, *Moses, From the Mysteries of Egypt to the Judges of Israel,* Floris Books, Edinburgh 1986.

Böhringer, Siegfried, *Astrologie,* Quell, Stuttgart 1990.

Brown, Pam, *Florence Nightingale,* Exley, Watford 1988.

Brunner-Traut, Emma, *Gelebte Mythen,* Wissenschaftliche Buchgesellschaft, Darmstadt 1981.

Choisnard, Paul, *Le méthode statique et le bon sens en astrologie,* 1896.

Christ, Felix, *Henry Dunant,* Friedrich Wittig, Hamburg 1979.

Clauss, Manfred, *Mithras, Kult und Mysterien,* C.H. Beck, Munich 1999.

Cumont, F., *Die Mysterien des Mithra,* Stuttgart 1923 (reprinted Darmstadt 1981).

Daems, Willem F., *Denn der Himmel ist der Mensch und der Mensch ist der Himmel – Paracelsia,* Philosophisch-Anthroposophischer Verlag, Dornach 1993.

—, *Streifzüge durch die Medizin- und Pharmaziegeschichte,* Verlag am Goetheanum, Dornach 2001.
Dietz, Karl-Martin, *Metamorphosen des Geistes, Beiträge zur Bewusstseinsgeschichte,* Vol. 4, 5 and 6, Freies Geistesleben, Stuttgart 1989/1990.
Dunant, Henry, *A Memory of Solferino,* International Committee of the Red Cross, 1986.
Faulkner, R.O., *The Ancient Egyptian Texts,* Clarendon Press, 1969.
Fischer, Hugo, *Die Geburt der Hochkultur in Ägypten und Mesopotamien,* Ernst Klett, Stuttgart 1960.
Floride, Athys, *Der Weg zu den Hierarchien; Das Ziel der Entwicklung: die vierte Hierarchie,* Verlag am Goetheanum, Dornach 1996.
Geissler, Horst Wolfram, *Astrologie, Geschichte, Entwicklung, Bedeutung,* Sanssouci, Zurich 1982.
Gleich, Sigismund, *see* von Gleich, Sigismund
Gsänger, Hans, *Mysteriengeschichte der Menschheit,* Die Kommenden, Freiburg 1971.
Harburger, W. (ed.) *Johannes Keplers 'Kosmische Harmonie',* Insel, Leipzig 1925.
Hemleben, Johannes, *Galileo Galilei,* Rowohlt, Hamburg 1969.
—, *Kepler in Selbstzeugnissen und Bilddokumenten,* Rowohlt, Hamburg 1971.
—, *Paracelsus – Revolutionär, Arzt und Christ,* Huber, Frauenfeld and Stuttgart 1973.
—, *Rudolf Steiner in Selbstzeugnissen und Bilddokumenten,* Rowohlt, Hamburg 1963.
Heudtlass, Willy, J. *Henry Dunant,* Kohlhammer, Stuttgart 1962.
Heymann, Dietrich, *see* Von Heymann, Dietrich
Hoppmann, Jürgen, G.H., *Astrologie der Reformationszeit,* Clemens Zerling, Berlin 1999.
Hornung, Erik, *Pharaonenzeit,* Deutscher Taschenbuch, Munich 1992.
Kaiser, Ernst, *Paracelsus in Selbstzeugnissen und Bilddokumenten,* Rowohlt, Hamburg 1969.
Knappich, Wilhelm, *Geschichte der Astrologie,* Vittorio Klostermann, Frankfurt am Main 1988.
Koch, Heinrich, *Michelangelo in Selbstzeugnissen und Bilddokumenten,* Rowohlt, Hamburg.
Kochanek, Hermann (ed.), *Horoskop als Schlüssel zum Ich, christlicher Glaube und Astrologie,* articles from a seminar on 'Astrology and Christian faith' at a college for missionaries in St Augustin, near Bonn, Germany, Verlagsgesellschaft Benno-Bernward-Morus 1995.
Kugler, F.X., *Sternkunde und Sterndienst in Babel,* Münster 1909.
Kuper, Michael, *Agrippa von Nettesheim, ein echter Faust,* Clemens Zerling, Berlin 1994.
Lehmann, Walther (ed.) *Heinrich Seuses deutsche Schriften,* 2 vols, Leipzig 1922.
Lindenberg, Christoph, *Rudolf Steiner, eine Biographie,* Freies Geistesleben, Stuttgart 1997.

Lusseyran, Jacques, *Against the Pollution of the I,* Morning Light Press, Idaho 2006.
—, *And There Was Light,* Floris Books, Edinburgh 1985.
—, *What One Sees Without Eyes,* Parabola Books, USA and Floris Books, Edinburgh 1999.
Macrobius, *Dream of Scipio.*
Morley, Henry, *Cornelius Agrippa: The Life of Henry Cornelius Agrippa von Nettesheim,* Chapman & Hall, London 1856.
Mulder, Elisabeth, *Sonne, Mond und Sterne,* Walter Keller, Dornach 1994.
Nadler, Steven, *Spinoza, a Life,* Cambridge University Press 2001.
Pannekoek, A., *A History of Astronomy,* Allen & Unwin, London 1961.
Paracelsus, *Die naturwissenschaftlichen und medizinischen Schriften des Paracelsus,* 14 Volumes, Karl Sudhoff, Munich 1922/23.
Parker, Derek and Julia, *A History of Astrology,* Harper Collins, London 1983.
Prokofieff, Sergei O., *Ewige Individualität; zur karmischen Novalis-Biographie,* Verlag am Goetheanum, Dornach 1987.
—, *Die geistigen Quellen Osteuropas und die künftigen Mysterien des Heiligen Gral,* Verlag am Goetheanum, Dornach 1989.
Ptolemy, Claudius, *Tetrabiblos,* compiled and edited by F. E. Robbins, Loeb Classical Library, Harvard University Press 1940.
Schad, Michael, *Paracelsus. Sein Ringen um eine wirklichkeitsgemässe Medizin,* Urachhaus, Stuttgart 1987.
Schäfer, Thomas, *Vom Sternenkult zur Astrologie,* Walther, Düsseldorf 1993.
Schütze, Alfred, *Mithras: Mysterien und Urchristentum,* Urachhaus, Stuttgart 1972.
Sementowsky-Kurillo, *see* von Sementowsky-Kurillo, Nicolaus
Servius, *Commentary on the Aeneid.*
Silesius, Angelus, *The Cherubinic Wanderer,* Paulist Press, New York 1986. —, *Selections from The Cherubinic Wanderer by Angelus Silesius,* Tr. J. E. Crawford Flitch, London, 1932.
Staubinger, Felix, *Du sollst keine anderen Götter neben mir haben,* self-published, Basel 1990.
Steiner, Rudolf, (CW = Complete Works, GA = Gesamtausgabe in German)
—, *Anthroposophical Leading Thoughts,* CW 26, Rudolf Steiner Press, UK 1998.
—, *Between Death and Rebirth,* GA 141, Rudolf Steiner Press, London 1975.
—, *Christ and the Spiritual World: The Search for the Holy Grail,* CW 149, Rudolf Steiner Press, UK 2008.
—, *Christus und die menschliche Seele,* GA 155.
—, *Cosmic Memory,* CW 11, Steinerbooks, USA 2006.
—, *Earthly Knowledge and Heavenly Wisdom,* CW 221, Anthroposophic Press, USA 1991.
—, *The East in the Light of the West,* CW 113, Anthropsophic Press, USA 1940.

—, *Esoteric Science, An Outline of,* CW 13, Anthropsophic Press, USA 1997 (also published as *Occult Science, an Outline,* Rudolf Steiner Press UK 2005).
—, *Esoterische Betrachtungen karmischer Zusammenhänge,* Vol. 5, GA 239, Dornach 1985.
—, *Eurythmy as Visible Speech,* CW 279, Rudolf Steiner Press, London, UK 1984.
—, *The Gospel of St Matthew,* CW 123, Rudolf Steiner Press, London, UK 1965.
—, *Human and Cosmic Thought,* CW 151, Anthroposophic Press, USA 1991.
—, *Initiationswissenschaft und Sternenerkenntnis,* GA 228, Dornach 1985
—, *The Karma of Untruthfulness,* Vol. 2, CW 174, Rudolf Steiner Press, UK 1992.
—, *Knowledge of the Higher Worlds, How is it Achieved?* CW 10. Rudolf Steiner Press, UK 2009.
—, *Life Between Death and Rebirth,* CW 140, Anthroposophic Press, USA 1968.
—, *Man's Being, his Destiny and World-evolution,* CW 226, Anthroposophic Press, USA 1984.
—, *Menschengeschichte im Lichte der Geistesforschung,* GA 61.
—, *The Mysteries of the East and of Christianity,* Anthroposophic Press, USA 1989.
—, *Die Mystik im Aufgange des neuzeitlichen Geisteslebens und ihr Verhältnis zur modernen Weltanschauung,* GA 7.
—, *Natur- und Geistwesen, ihr Wirken in unserer sichtbaren Welt,* GA 98.
—, *The New Spirituality and the Christ Experience of the Twentieth Century,* CW 200, Rudolf Steiner Press, London, UK 1988.
—, *Occult Science, an Outline,* CW 13, Rudolf Steiner Press, UK 1963.
—, *Rosicrucianism and Modern Initiation,* CW 233, Anthroposophic Press, USA 1982.
—, *The Spiritual Guidance of the Individual and Humanity,* CW 15, Anthroposophic Press, USA 1992.
—, *The Stages of Higher Knowledge,* CW 12, Steinerbooks, USA 2009.
—, *Theosophy, An Introduction to the Supersensible Knowledge of the World and the Destination of Man,* CW 9, Steinerbooks, USA 2005.
—, *Verses and Meditations,* Rudolf Steiner Press, UK 2004.
—, *Zeitgeschichtliche Betrachtungen,* GA 174.
Störig, Hans Joachim, *Geschiedenis van de filosofie,* Prisma, Amsterdam 1959.
Strauss, H. A. and Strauss-Kloebe, S., *Die Astrologie des Johannes Kepler,* Adolf Bonz, Fellbach-Oeffingen 1981.
Sucher, Willi O., *Cosmic Christianity and the Changing Countenance of Cosmology,* Steiner Books, USA 1993.
—, *Isis Sophia II: Outline of a New Star Wisdom,* Astrosophy Research Center, USA, and Anastasi, UK 2000.

Teichmann, Frank, *Die ägyptischen Mysterien, Quellen einer Hochkultur,* Freies Geistesleben, Stuttgart 1999.
—, *Die Kultur der Empfindungsseele,* Freies Geistesleben, Stuttgart 1990.
—, *Die Kultur der Verstandesseele,* Freies Geistesleben, Stuttgart 1993.
Thieben, Ludwig, *Das Rätsel des Judentums,* Perseus, Basel 1991.
Thomas Aquinas, *The Summa Theologica of St Thomas Aquinas,* Bibliolife 2009.
Thompson, R.C. *The Reports of the Magicians and Astrologers of Nineveh and Babylon,* 1900.
Uehli, Ernst, *Kultur und Kunst Ägyptens, ein Isisgeheimnis,* Philosophisch-Anthroposophischer Verlag, Dornach 1955.
Ungnad, Arthur, *Die Religion der Babylonier und Assyrer,* Eugen Diederichts, Jena 1921.
Vetter, Suso, *Das Geburtshoroskop der Welt,* Verlag am Goetheanum, Dornach 1993.
Vloemans, A., *Inleiding tot Spinoza,* van Stockum en Zoon, The Hague 1953.
Voltmer, Ulrieke, *Rhythmische Astrologie, Johannes Keplers Prognose-Methode aus neuer Sicht,* Urania, Neuhausen am Rheinfall 1997.
Von Heymann, Dietrich, *Wo ist der rote Faden? Leben zwischen Astrologie und Glauben,* Wittnau 1988.
von Gleich, Sigismund, *Marksteine der Kulturgeschichte,* Mellinger Verlag, Stuttgart 1982.
von Sementowsky-Kurillo, Nicolaus, *Der Mensch griff nach den Sternen,* Werner Classen, Zurich 1970.
Voss, Gerhard, *Astrologie christlich,* Friedrich Pustet, Regensburg 1980.
Waage, Peter Normann, *Der unsichtbare Kontinent; Wladimir Solowjow, der Denker Europas,* Freies Geistesleben, Stuttgart 1988.
Wegener, Günther S., *6000 Jahre und ein Buch,* Oncken Verlag, Wuppertal and Kassel 1992.
Winkel, Erich (ed.) *Ptolemy, Claudius, Tetrabiblos, nach der von Philipp Melanchthon besorgten seltenen Ausgabe aus dem Jahre 1553.* Chiron, Mössingen 1995.
Wir erlebten Rudolf Steiner. Erinnerungen seiner Schüler. Verlag Freies Geistesleben, Stuttgart (1967),
Wirken Rudolf Steiners, Das, Volume 3: 1907 to 1917, Novalis, Munich.
Wolfram, Elise, *Der esoterische Christ Paracelsus,* Philosophisch-Anthroposophischer Verlag, Dornach 1991.
—, *Die okkulten Ursachen der Krankheiten: Volumen Paramirum,* ed. Willem F. Daems, Philosophisch-Anthroposophischer Verlag, Dornach 1991.
Woodham-Smith, Cecil, *Florence Nightingale,* Penguin.
Zeylmans van Emmichoven, F.W., *Die Wirklichkeit, in der wir leben,* Verlag am Goetheanum, Dornach 1977.

Index